$14.36　　　　　　　　　　　c.1　　　　　　　　　　　7

Model a MONSTER

Model a
MONSTER

Making dinosaurs from everyday materials

Colin Caket

Blandford Press
Poole New York Sydney

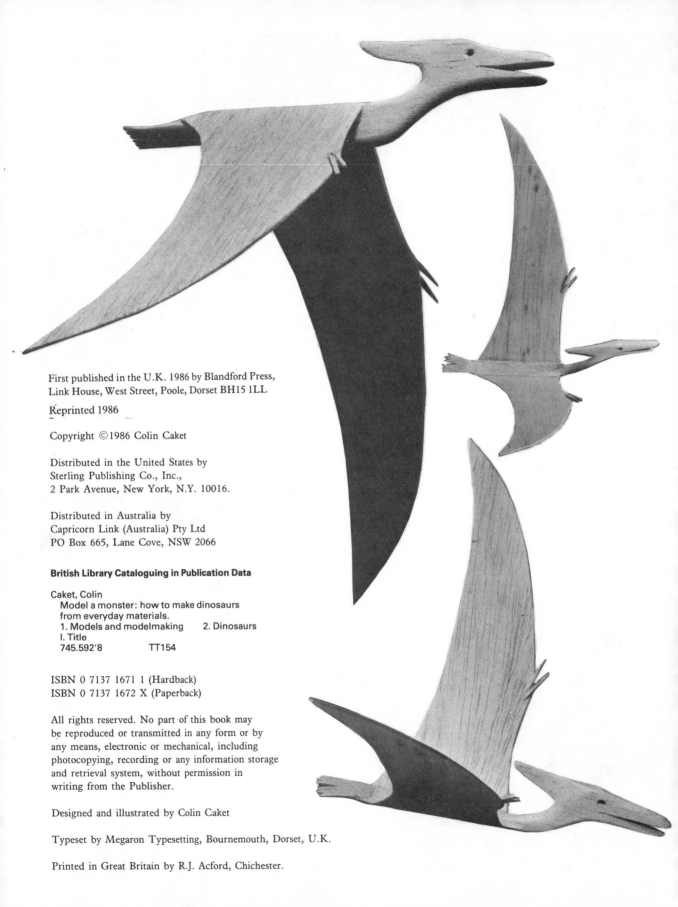

First published in the U.K. 1986 by Blandford Press,
Link House, West Street, Poole, Dorset BH15 1LL

Reprinted 1986

Distributed in the United States by
Sterling Publishing Co., Inc.,
2 Park Avenue, New York, N.Y. 10016.

Distributed in Australia by
Capricorn Link (Australia) Pty Ltd
PO Box 665, Lane Cove, NSW 2066

British Library Cataloguing in Publication Data

Caket, Colin
   Model a monster: how to make dinosaurs
   from everyday materials.
   1. Models and modelmaking   2. Dinosaurs
   I. Title
   745.592'8   TT154

ISBN 0 7137 1671 1 (Hardback)
ISBN 0 7137 1672 X (Paperback)

Designed and illustrated by Colin Caket

Typeset by Megaron Typesetting, Bournemouth, Dorset, U.K.

Printed in Great Britain by R.J. Acford, Chichester.

Contents

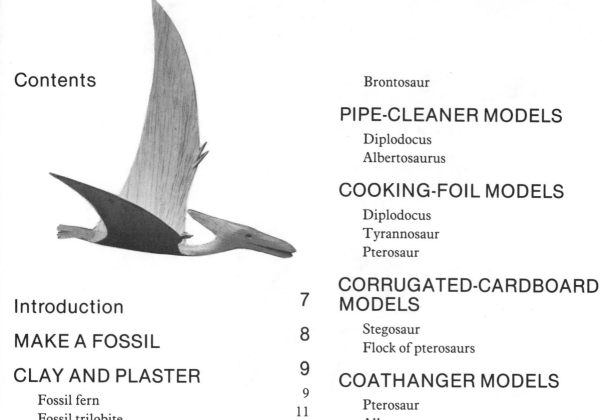

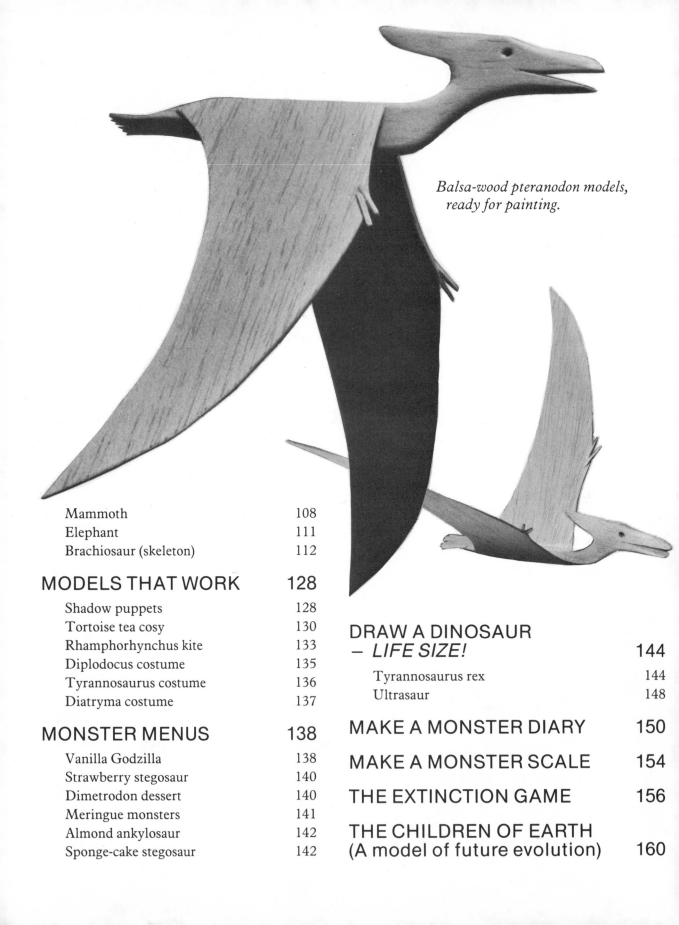

Balsa-wood pteranodon models, ready for painting.

Introduction

With this book and a bit of practice you will be able to make interesting and life-like models of prehistoric animals. The materials and tools suggested aren't hard to find, expensive or difficult to use. A list of what you will need heads each project. Imagination *isn't* listed, but you could use a little of that too.

An elephant's long trunk and ears like car doors would be unknown to us if we had only its skeleton to study. So would a zebra's stripes and a leopard's spots. Apart from a few footprints, all we know about most prehistoric animals has been guessed at from their fossilized bones. Just think what strange trunks and tentacles, patterns and colours we might see if only we could go back in time and study the living animals. That's where the imagination comes in.

Most of the models in this book are of animals which date from the period of the dinosaurs. At any one time there must have been as great a variety of dinosaurs as there is of mammals now, and different species undoubtedly lumbered, trotted or sprinted through the various ages and environments of the dinosaurs' long rule.

When we look at reconstructed dinosaur skeletons we see two basic patterns, those who walked on two legs (far more walked erect than do mammals) and those who walked on four. But there is endless variety in their size, weight and the length of their limbs, tails and necks. Some of them, like the armoured ankylosaurus with a tail like a mace, stegosaurus with a double frill of bony plates from head to tail and triceratops with its three horns, left fossil evidence of these features. Some things can be calculated by comparison with living animals, but there are no exact equivalents so there is always more work to be done. With new discoveries and techniques in palaeontology, and fresh ideas about the nature of prehistoric life – the past has never had a better future!

Even after you have made all the models in this book you will have only started on the endless possibilities of the subject.

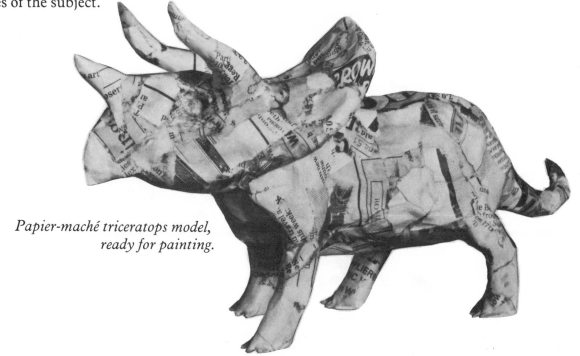

Papier-maché triceratops model, ready for painting.

Make a fossil

What is the hardest substance in your body? Quite right, tooth enamel. Hands up all those who said bone. Well, bone is the next hardest, so you were *nearly* right. This is true of many other animals as well as us. After they died, the teeth and bones of ancient animals usually lasted much longer than the rest of their bodies, so teeth and bones are the bits which most often managed to get fossilized.

The mud or sand surrounding these remains slowly turned into rock when a massive weight of sediment accumulated on top of it. Fossils are not usually the actual bones or teeth themselves. More often their substance has been gradually replaced by minerals in solution in water oozing through the rock, and they also have turned into rock, but rock of a different hardness or colour, so their shape is preserved, sometimes in microscopic detail. The surrounding stone might break cleanly away, more often it has to be dissolved in acid or painstakingly removed with tools like dentist's drills before the fossil can be seen.

The bones and teeth could get widely scattered, but enough are sometimes found together to re-assemble a complete skeleton, giving an idea of what the living animal looked like.

Some animals don't have teeth, or even bones, and plants certainly don't have either. We find plenty of fossilized shells, and the hard parts of insects, as well as spines and scales and feathers and leaves and cones and nuts and roots and other bits and pieces. In the right conditions even footprints in mud can get fossilized, if they happen to get filled with volcanic ash or drifting sand. Buried for millions of years, these turn into different kinds of stone, and the footprints can reappear when the upper layer finally gets weathered away again.

Making a fossil is quite easy, but it requires patience. All you have to do is to bury something in a swamp, taking careful note of exactly where you buried it, and then dig it up a few million years later. If you can't be bothered to wait you will just have to *fake* a fossil. You can do so quite easily with clay and plaster, and get a very lifelike result too (if lifelike is the right word for a fossil).

*Fossils of trilobites
from North and South America*

Clay and plaster

The best type of clay to use is 'potter's clay' (bought in bags from schools' suppliers or potters' suppliers). If you are lucky though, you can dig up clay in your garden. If not, thick mud is a reasonable substitute. Sieve bits of twig, stones and so on from some soil and stir in a little water till it is well mixed. It should be about the consistency of cream cheese.

The plaster you need is called plaster of Paris, which is pure white and goes directly from a liquid to a solid state (getting quite warm in the process because of the chemical reaction).

FOSSIL FERN

You will need:
A board to work on
Clay (or soil and a fine mesh sieve)
A rolling pin, bottle or strong cardboard tube
(*or* another board to press the clay flat)
Plaster of Paris
Water
A bowl or bucket to mix the plaster in
A spoon or stick to stir with
A frond of fern

1. Roll a lump of clay flat on the board.

2. Spread the fern flat, then press it into the surface with the roller.

3. Lift up the stem, then peel the fern off, leaving an impression in the clay.

9

4. Carefully build a wall from more clay all round it. It has to be thick and strong enough to hold the plaster until it sets.

5. Mix plaster in water to about the consistency of thin cream.

6. Pour the plaster carefully into one corner so it runs over the surface—filling up the impression of the fern.

7. When you have poured in the plaster, lift a corner of the board a little and drop it to shake out any bubbles.

8. When the plaster sets, turn it over and roll back the clay. Keep the clay in a plastic bag to use again later.

9. Wash off any remaining clay with a soft brush. You can paint or varnish the plaster when it's dry.

FOSSIL TRILOBITE

Trilobites were hard-shelled animals which lived beneath the seas of five hundred million years ago, when the land was still barren. Many of the creatures in those seas would look strange to us, but things like starfish and jellyfish haven't much changed, even today.

As well as clay and plaster etc, you will need:

A pencil
Tracing paper
Scissors
Some corrugated cardboard
A thimble (optional)

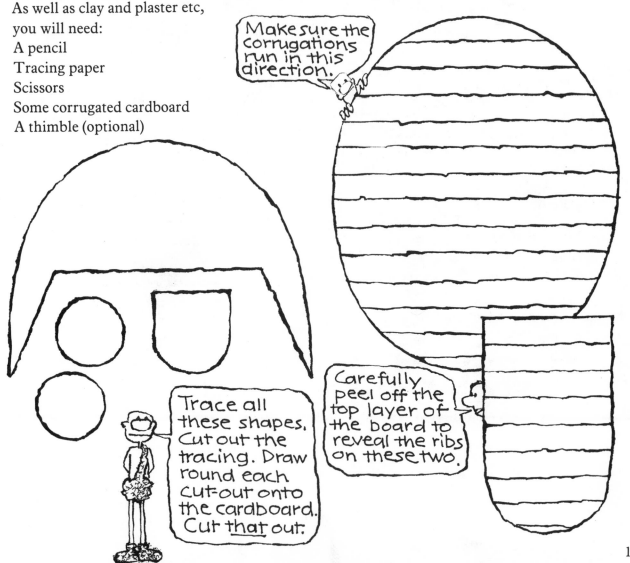

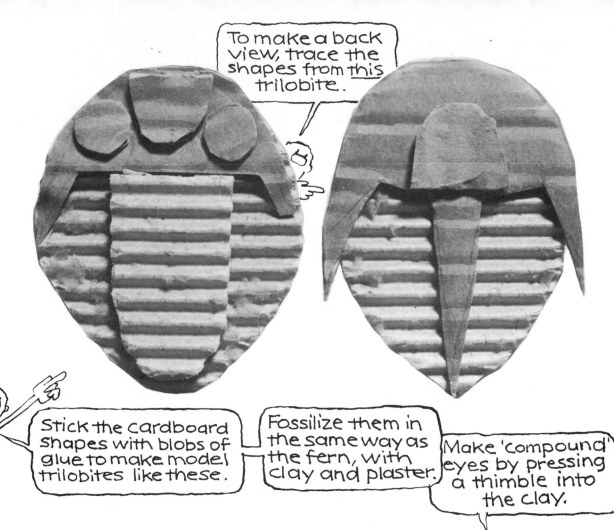

To make a back view, trace the shapes from this trilobite.

Stick the cardboard shapes with blobs of glue to make model trilobites like these.

Fossilize them in the same way as the fern, with clay and plaster.

Make 'compound' eyes by pressing a thimble into the clay.

FOSSIL SERPENT

You will *also* need:

About a yard (1 m) of string

A small piece of corrugated cardboard

Scissors

A hole punch (optional)

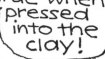

You can make ribs and a backbone from string like this. The knots make great vertebrae when pressed into the clay!

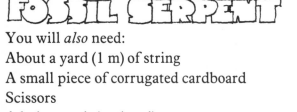

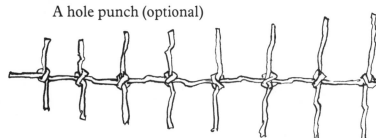

Cut a skull from corrugated cardboard. Use a hole punch to cut the eyes.

FOSSIL AMMONITE

The fossilized shells of ancient ammonites, some of them very large, were at first taken for coiled snakes – which seemed to support legends of sea serpents. The bones of huge extinct animals encouraged rumours of giants and dragons. Modern investigators have added flesh to these bones in a more scientific way, sending sea serpents and dragons back to the realms of myth. Fossil snakes *have* been found, but ammonites they aren't!

You will *also* need:
Some old cloth or thin felt
About a yard (1 m) of braid or cord
Scissors

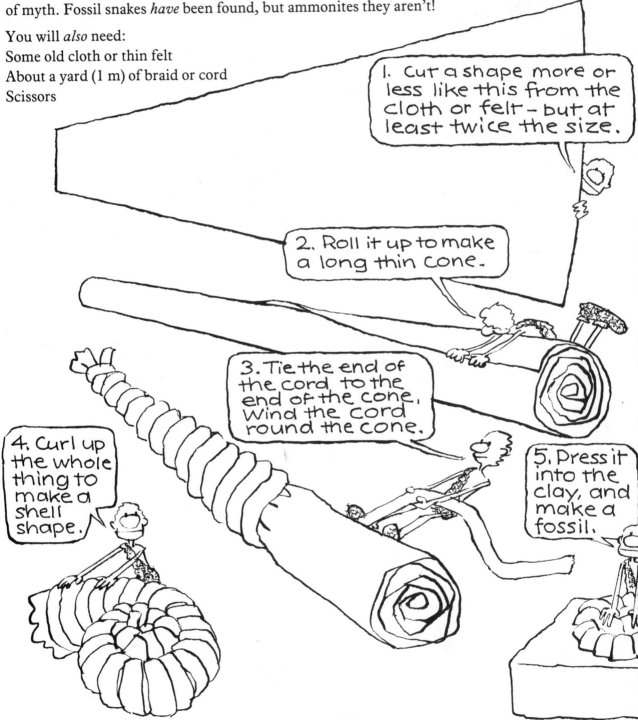

1. Cut a shape more or less like this from the cloth or felt – but at least twice the size.

2. Roll it up to make a long thin cone.

3. Tie the end of the cord to the end of the cone. Wind the cord round the cone.

4. Curl up the whole thing to make a shell shape.

5. Press it into the clay, and make a fossil.

Plasticine and modelling clays

A variety of products specially designed for modelling are sold in toy-shops and department stores. Most come in sets of different colours and are re-usable. When taking old models apart you have to separate the colours very carefully or they soon go muddy. The models made of one product can be made permanent in an oven. Another type hardens in air in a few hours. This kind has to be painted if you want your model coloured.

All types hold their shapes and take detail well. Parts can be modelled separately and stuck together. Your fingers are all that is essential for modelling, but a few simple tools are useful too. These might include a board to work on, a dinner knife, a teaspoon, a pencil, a toothpick and a large nail. Toothpicks and bent nails can also become parts of a model, standing in for things like horns or tusks. Some cooking foil or plastic sheet is useful to stand the stuff on or to wrap up any left over, as it can leave greasy marks.

The unused part of the air-hardening type has to be wrapped up especially carefully to exclude air, for obvious reasons. This type is ideal for fleshing out and adding details to larger models made from papier-maché. Otherwise small models are best because these products are expensive in large quantities.

14

DIPLODOCUS

Roll out one ball and three sausages. Cut one sausage into four to make the legs. The other two make the neck and tail, and the ball is the body of this model diplodocus.

The diplodocus was a sort of sports version of the brontosaurus, being longer and thinner, with a much more extended neck and tail. The diplodocus was one of the longest and the brontosaurus one of the heaviest animals ever to live.

The diplodocus had the smallest brain in relation to its size of any known vertebrate (animal with a backbone). Like many other large dinosaurs it had a nerve centre in its rear that was actually larger than its brain. This was once thought to *be* a second brain.

It was also once thought that these animals were too big to have lived on land, and that their legs would have collapsed under the great weight of their bodies if these weren't buoyed up by water. It was supposed that they used their long necks like periscopes in order to breathe while they walked on the bottoms of rivers and lakes.

Now it has been calculated that it would be beyond the power of any known type of animal muscle to inflate a rib cage under such a weight of water. It seems, after all, that these animals walked on land, and used their long necks to browse off the tops of trees, like a modern giraffe. If so, they could have reached leaves three times higher than those nibbled by a giraffe!

MAMMOTH

TYRANNOSAUR

The great advantage of modelling clay is that you can take bits off and stick bits back on until you eventually get the shape right. Getting the shape right is what is most important. Don't worry too much about getting a smooth finish, a smooth finish will tend to make your model look dull and uninteresting.

ARCHAEOPTERYX

You will *also* need:

Some small feathers (these aren't always easy to find, but can usually be bought from schools' suppliers in packs, or in bags from drapers, or from a butcher selling game)

Model a small dinosaur of the kind which stood on two legs – *don't* use the sort of modelling material which has to be hardened in an oven! Stick a line of feathers in each side of the tail, and rows of feathers over the body and arms. Make each row just overlap the last. Start at the rear and work your way towards the front. Leave the face and feet bald. This is a model of archaeopteryx.

The archaeopteryx fossils are said to be the most valuable of all. The animal is a rare 'missing link' from a stage in evolution when one thing is changing into another, with features from both – in this case feathers (which no reptile has) and teeth (which no bird has). Some scientists argue that birds *are* dinosaurs. If so, you can even *dine* on a dinosaur! Do you doubt it? Take a close look at a hen's feet!

If you can't get the feathers in easily, make holes first and press the point of each feather into a hole.

Sand and snow modelling

Don't just make sand castles on the beach – model sand monsters too! You can make quite subtle shapes from damp sand, but it is best to work on a fairly large scale. Avoid undercutting too much, or the section above might collapse. Scratch the outline shape on a flat bit of sand first. Don't start digging for material *too* close or half your model might slide into the hole. Start work when the tide is going out! Use stones or shells for details like eyes or toes.

These designs can be made just as well from snow in winter. Roll up two or three large snowballs to collect modelling material. You might think Ice Age animals a more appropriate subject. If so think out some designs for yourself. Don't forget that you can undercut snow a *little* more easily than sand, to make a gap between a mammoth's stumpy legs, for example. But the end of his trunk had better rest on the ground, or it might fall off, and his tusks had better be made from sticks or carrots or something.

You will need:
A sandy beach or a large sand pit (fine sand is better than coarse)
Spades (as large as you can easily handle)
Buckets (to move sand in)
A watering can (to keep your model damp without washing it away)
A trowel (for fine modelling)
A brush, broom or rake (for smoothing)
Some friends to help (with bigger models)
A camera (to record your masterpiece)
A plastic bag (to put the camera *in* to keep the sand *out*)
Warm clothes (for the snow-modelling version)

If you have a friend with another spade, get the mound moved a bit further away from the hole.

With sand, think big. Maybe not life-sized, but big. Start with a hole and a mound.

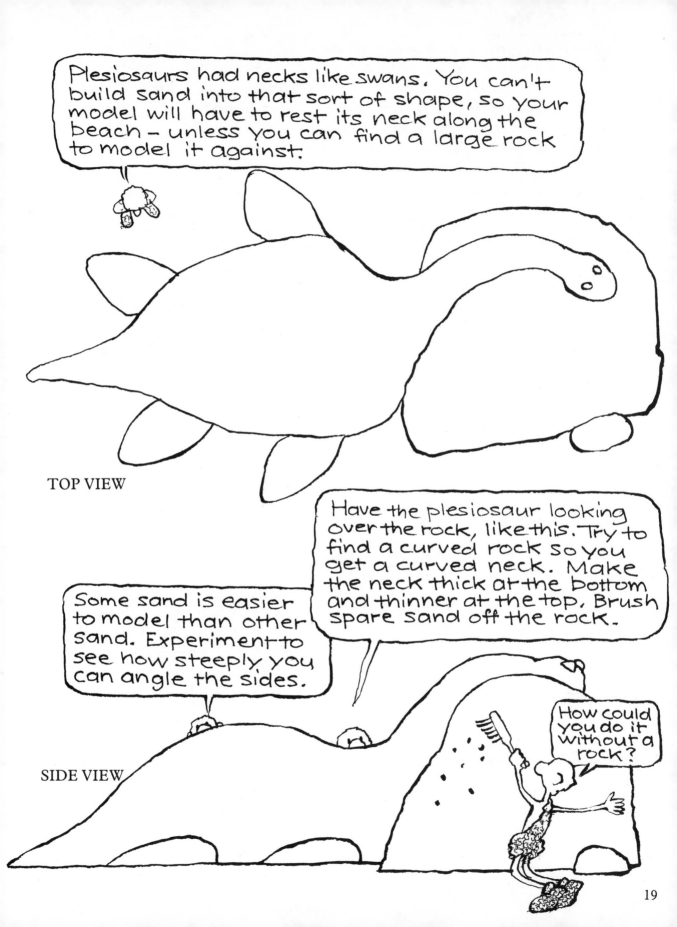

Plesiosaurs had necks like swans. You can't build sand into that sort of shape, so your model will have to rest its neck along the beach — unless you can find a large rock to model it against.

TOP VIEW

Have the plesiosaur looking over the rock, like this. Try to find a curved rock so you get a curved neck. Make the neck thick at the bottom and thinner at the top. Brush spare sand off the rock.

Some sand is easier to model than other sand. Experiment to see how steeply you can angle the sides.

SIDE VIEW

How could you do it without a rock?

19

Another contemporary of the dinosaurs was the ichthyosaur. You wouldn't have expected to see one on a beach very often because it bore its young alive, at sea. Different species ranged in size from that of a modern dolphin to that of a killer whale (which is a large species of dolphin). Ichthyosaurs lived a very similar life-style to dolphins and they closely resembled a dolphin in appearance. This is called 'convergent evolution'.

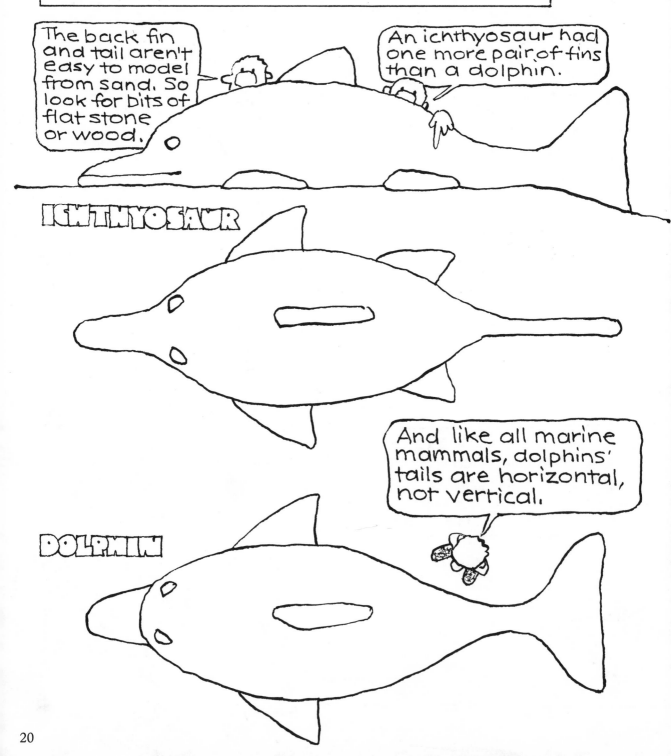

The back fin and tail aren't easy to model from sand. So look for bits of flat stone or wood.

An ichthyosaur had one more pair of fins than a dolphin.

ICHTHYOSAUR

And like all marine mammals, dolphins' tails are horizontal, not vertical.

DOLPHIN

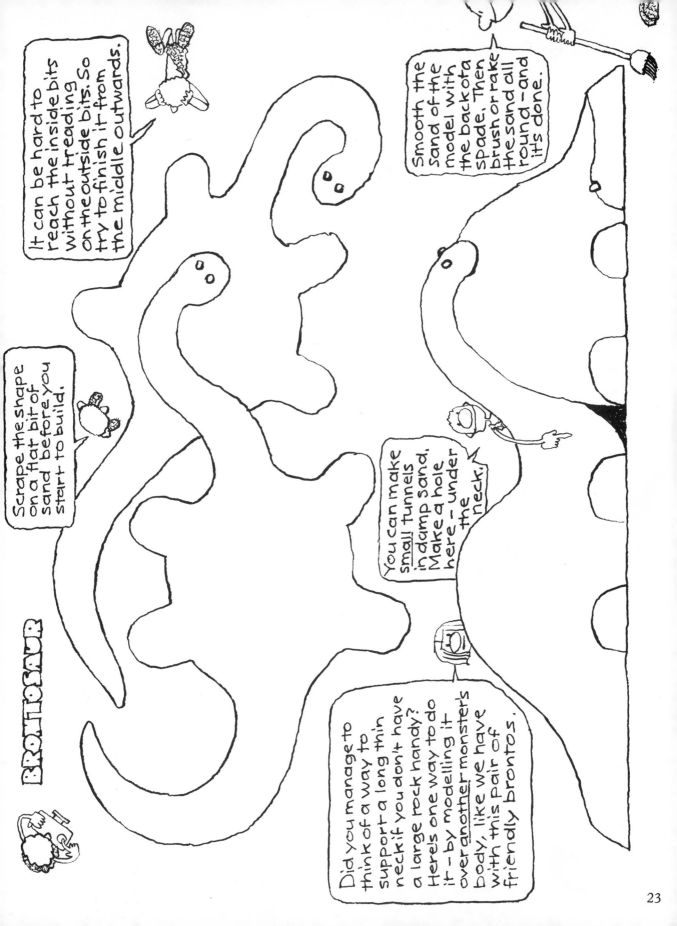

BRONTOSAUR

It can be hard to reach the inside bits without treading on the outside bits. So try to finish it from the middle outwards.

Smooth the sand of the model with the back of a spade. Then brush or rake the sand all round – and it's done.

Scrape the shape on a flat bit of sand before you start to build.

You can make small tunnels in damp sand. Make a hole here – under the neck.

Did you manage to think of a way to support a long thin neck if you don't have a large rock handy? Here's one way to do it – by modelling it over another monster's body, like we have with this pair of friendly brontos.

23

Pipe-cleaner models

Pipe-cleaners can be bought from tobacconists. They are also made in all sorts of colours especially for modelling. They can be cut with scissors to shorten them, or twisted together to extend them. They can be wound round a pencil to make short tubes or coils, or round and round each other to make solid shapes. Whatever shape they are twisted into they stay in.

You will need:
A packet or two of pipe-cleaners
Scissors
A pencil

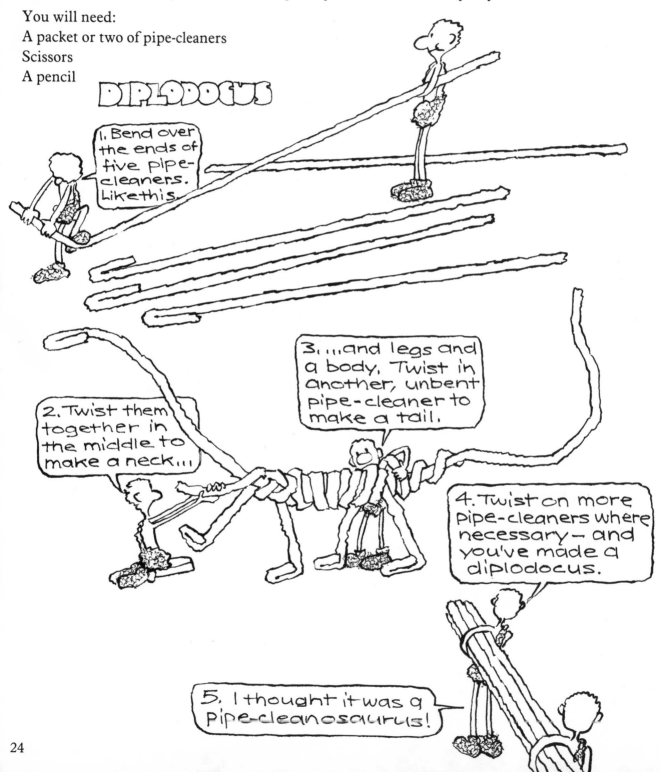

DIPLODOCUS

1. Bend over the ends of five pipe-cleaners. Like this.

2. Twist them together in the middle to make a neck....

3. ....and legs and a body. Twist in another, unbent pipe-cleaner to make a tail.

4. Twist on more pipe-cleaners where necessary — and you've made a diplodocus.

5. I thought it was a pipe-cleanosaurus!

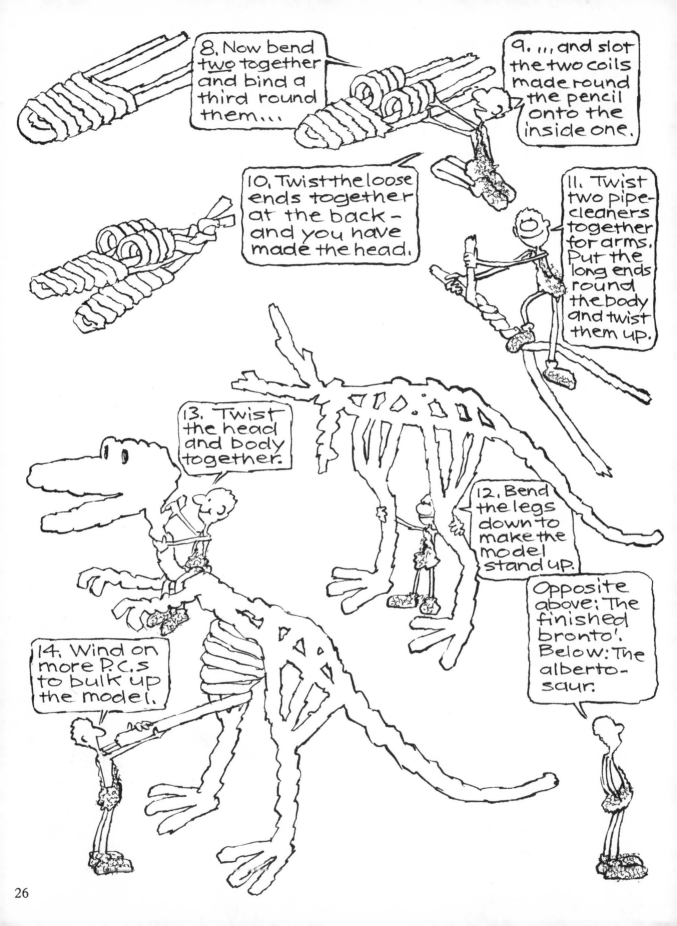

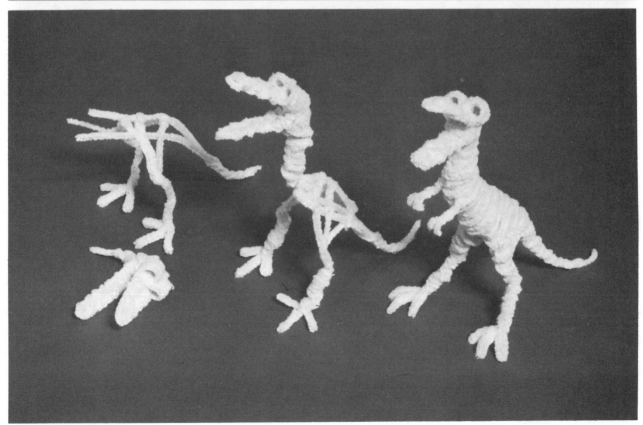

1. Unroll a length of cooking foil about three times the width and cut it off.

3. ...at both ends - like this.

Cooking-foil models

Buy cooking foil in rolls at least 23½ inches (60 cm) wide. Get the widest size you can – the models that you make will come out smaller than you might expect.

Cooking foil is so adaptable you can make long, thin shapes or short, fat shapes from the same basic rectangle. You can even add strips of foil if you need to make the body fatter or the tail longer. Just tear off another strip and crumple it and the original piece together.

You can make quite differently-shaped prehistoric animals from the same basic pattern of a longish rectangle with some slits in each end. Don't scrunch the foil down too tightly until you are ready to add the finishing touches. The more tightly compressed foil is, the more difficult it is to model with or to alter.

Cooking foil is just a thin sheet of a very pliable and light, but strong, metal. The longest, thinnest bits of your model should stay put without support.

2. Make two cuts about one third of the length...

4. Crumple up the foil from both ends towards the middle.

You will need:
A roll of cooking foil (keep the cardboard roll it comes on – it will be useful later)
Scissors

5. Make the middle strip long and thin. The outer strips shorter and thicker.

6. Finally crumple up the middle to form the body of your diplodocus.

With a little practice you will be able to make lots of other monsters from the same basic pattern.

Who are you calling a monster?

You might have seen cartoons, or even feature films, of cavemen like me battling with dinosaurs. The dinosaurs all disappeared about seventy million years ago. Nothing you or I would care to recognise as a relative has been around for even as long as three per cent of that time. So they would never have met a dinosaur in a million years (or rather *two* million years)!

Dinosaurs are sometimes called '*Prehistoric* Monsters'. That must be the understatement of all time. Recorded history started about five thousand years ago. The dinosaurs vanished from the Earth no less than fourteen thousand times longer ago than that. How prehistoric can you get!

29

TYRANNOSAUR

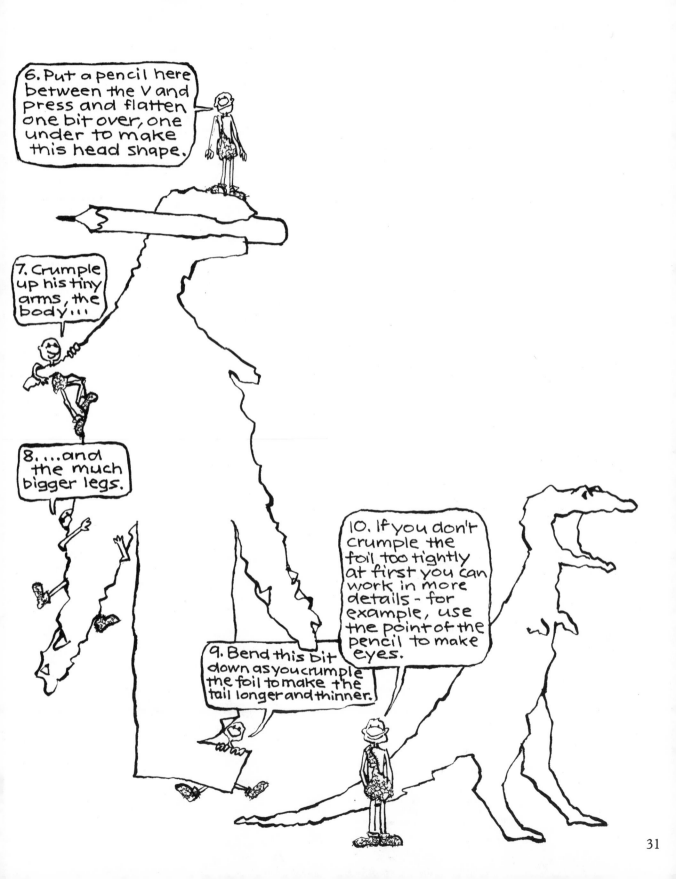

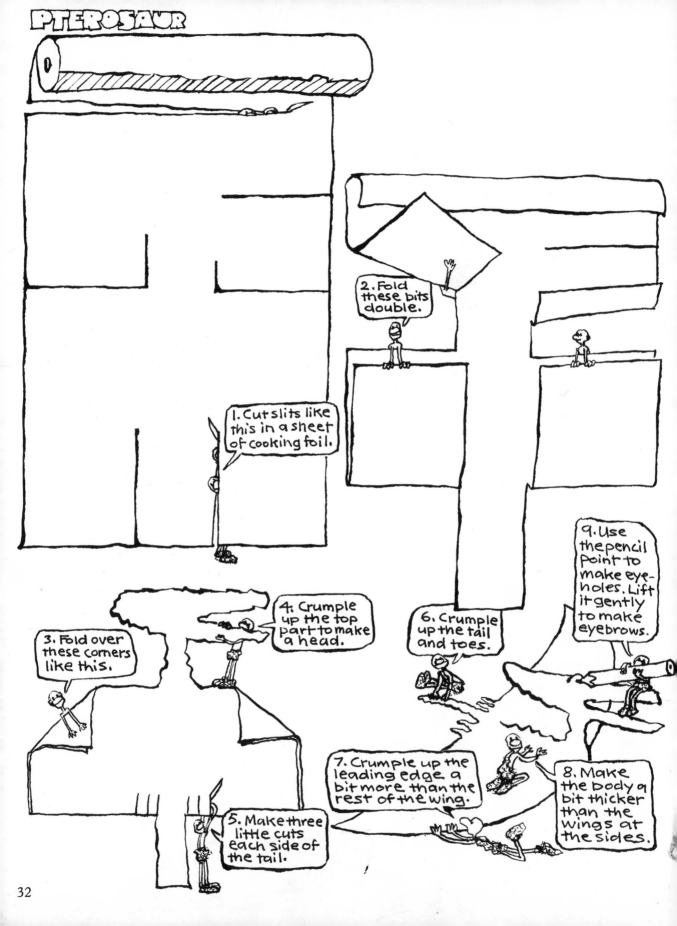

PTEROSAUR

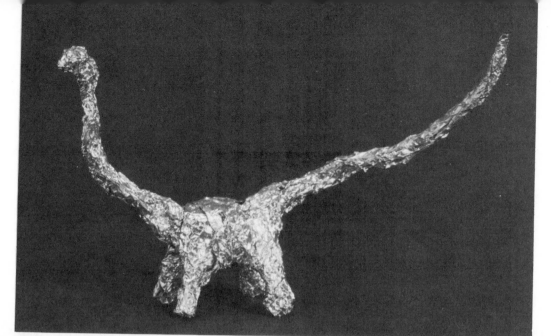

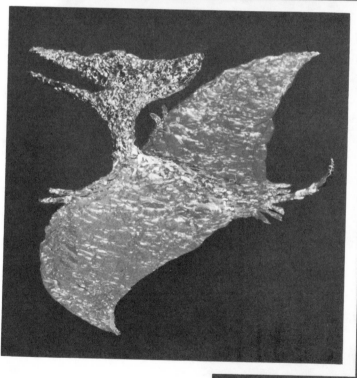

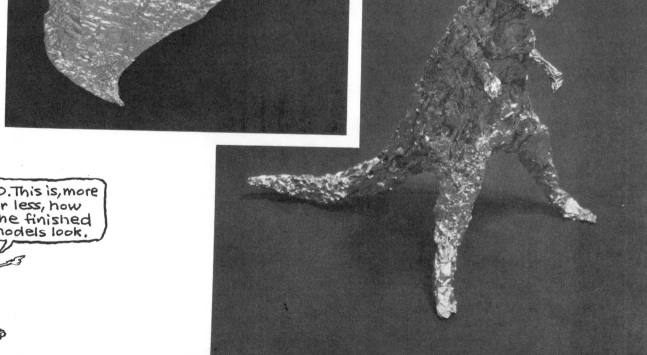

10. This is, more or less, how the finished models look.

Corrugated-cardboard models

Corrugated cardboard is lighter and much easier to cut than ordinary cardboard.
It can be scavenged from used boxes and packing material. It comes in different weights and
thicknesses. If what you are using is hard to cut, look for some thinner stuff. It should cut
easily with scissors, but there are two other ways to get into difficult corners. You can
use a fretsaw (cardboard clogs the teeth more than wood, use an old toothbrush to clean them)
or you can use a craft knife. Craft knives are, or should be, *sharp*. They will cut fingers and
table tops as well as cardboard, so use them with care. Fingers heal, table tops don't,
so always place some plywood or thick cardboard under what you are cutting. *Don't* use more
corrugated cardboard. It cuts through too easily! Corrugated cardboard will compress,
which makes it easy to slot two pieces together in a firm joint. With thicker boards, you might
have to make two parallel cuts close together and pull out the thin strip between in order
to make the slot sufficiently wide. It makes it easier to fold accurately if you go over the fold
first with a *blunt* knife against a ruler, this is called 'scoring'. (A *sharp* knife will cut
right through!) Corrugated cardboard models are easy to paint with powder paints, poster
paints or acrylic paints.

You will need:
A large sheet or two of corrugated cardboard
A soft pencil (about 4B)
A ruler
A blunt knife (for scoring)
Scissors (possibly also a fretsaw or a craft knife)
A pin or a pair of compasses
A board (to work on)
Powder, poster or acrylic paints
Brushes
A coathanger and a needle and thread (for the flock of pteranodons)

34

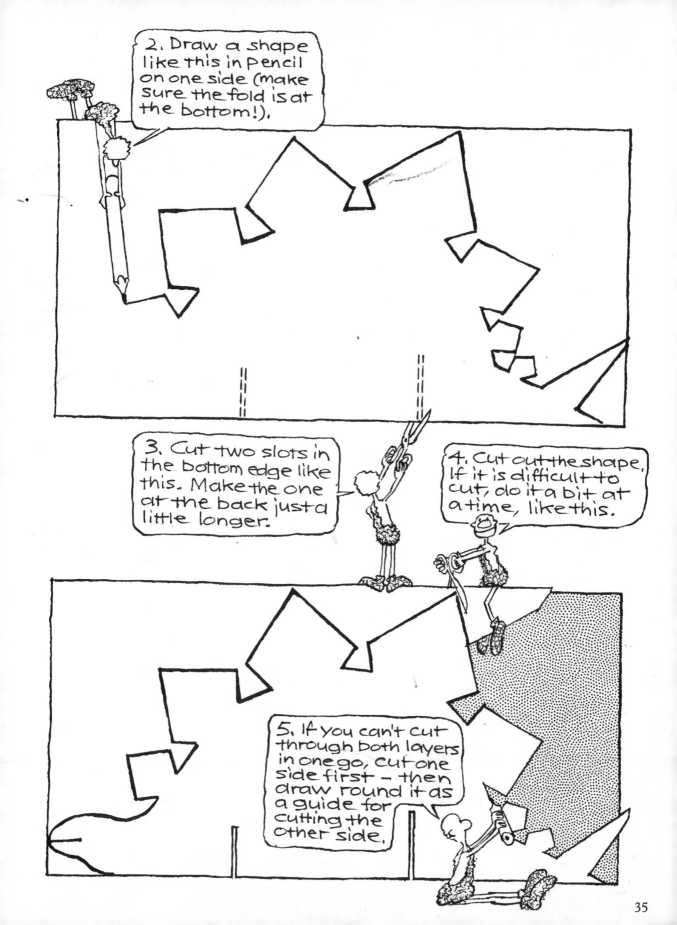

2. Draw a shape like this in pencil on one side (make sure the fold is at the bottom!).

3. Cut two slots in the bottom edge like this. Make the one at the back just a little longer.

4. Cut out the shape. If it is difficult to cut, do it a bit at a time, like this.

5. If you can't cut through both layers in one go, cut one side first – then draw round it as a guide for cutting the other side.

35

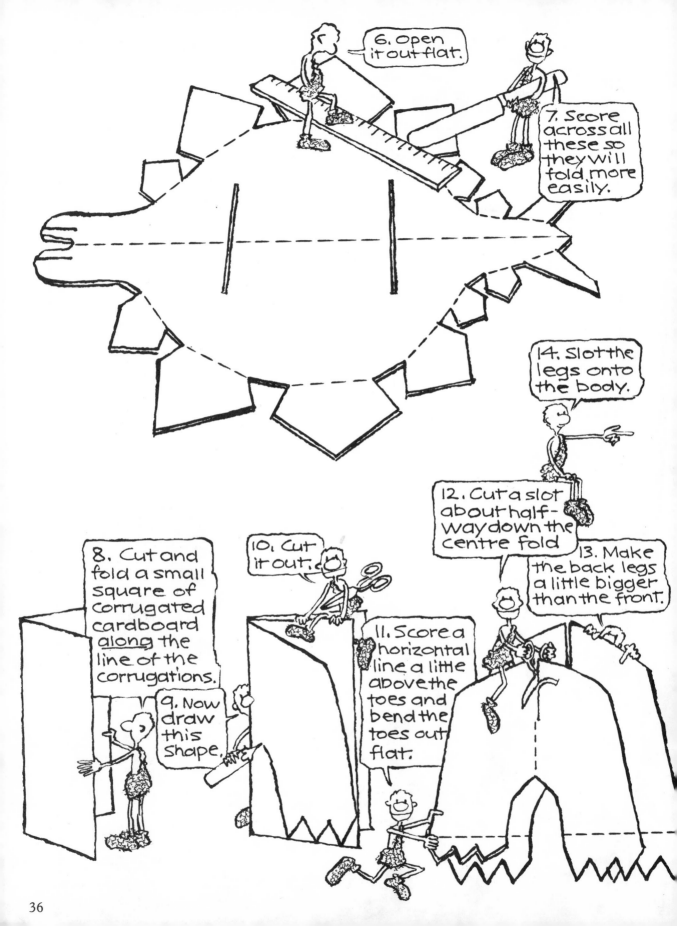

15. Spread the 'bony plates' on the back apart a bit. Then make the eyes with the point of a pencil.

16. Then all you have to do is to paint it.

What colour? All we know about dinosaurs we have found out from their fossilized bones. Who would guess, looking at the skeleton of a tiger, that its hide is so stripey? Nobody knows what patterns and colours decorated the dinosaurs, so you will have to use your imagination.

Some living reptiles are very brightly coloured, so it is possible that dinosaurs were too, though they aren't very closely related.

Perhaps some species were green. For some reason there are virtually no green mammals (except for a few which have plants growing on them) and there are only a few green birds. But it would be a logical colour for both a predator stalking prey *and* for prey trying not to be too conspicuous in vegetation.

Some modern lizards are green. Maybe dinosaurs were?

17. This is what your unpainted model will look like.

FLOCK OF PTEROSAURS

Scavenge another box or two.

Draw a body and head for every set of wings. Vary the mouths a bit.

Work this size.

Draw about ten wing shapes like this onto board and cut them out.

With the thicker type of corrugated cardboard make two parallel cuts and remove the strip in between.

Start the eye-holes with the point of a compass.

Enlarge the holes with a pencil point.

Slot each set of wings onto a body.

Look at the wire hanger. What does it's shape suggest?

Find the point of balance in the back of the head with the compasses. Thread cotton through it, and hang it from the hanger.

Use the corners of old boxes to make some of the wings go up or down.

39

Coathanger models

Did you realise before that pteranodons were not extinct, but hang like bats in flocks in the darkness of wardrobes in cheap hotels?

You will need:

Wire coathangers

A few pipe-cleaners (to make fingers and toes)

Cardboard tubes (such as those from the middle of rolls of paper towels etc.)

Clothes pegs or spring grips

P.V.A. (white) glue

A bowl (to dilute the glue in with a little water)

Another bowl (to rinse your fingers in)

A cloth (to wipe your fingers clean)

Plenty of old newspapers

A roll of masking tape

Scissors

Some modelling clay of the kind which dries in air (optional)

About twenty carpet tacks (for teeth)

Paints and a brush

PTEROSAUR

Thin some glue in a bowl with a little water when you are ready to start dipping strips of newspaper into it. Don't overthin it.

Bend up the end of the coathanger, like this.

Lift up each 'wing' of the coathanger like this.

Cut a shorter slot on top at one end.

Cut off a length of the cardboard tube a bit longer than the line A to B. Then cut a slot at each side and at each end.

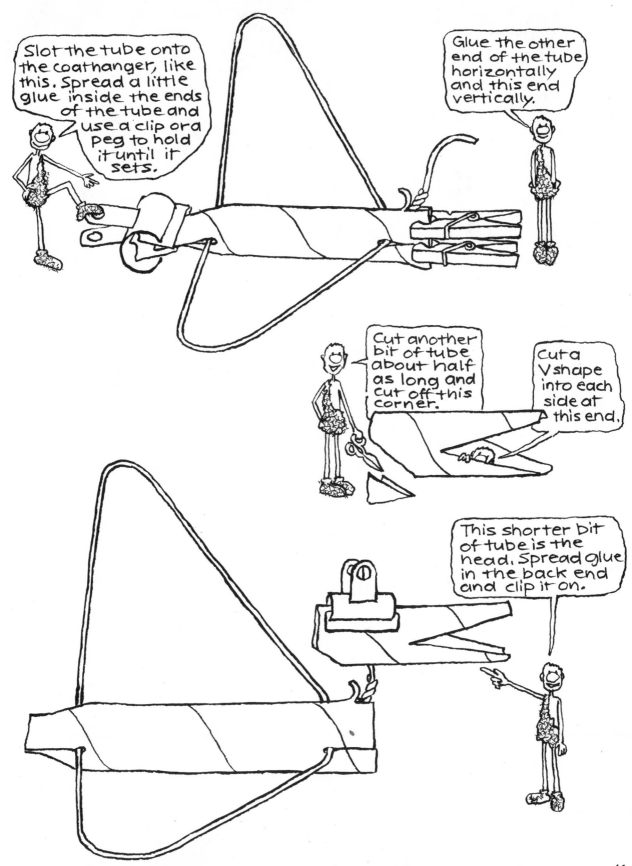

41

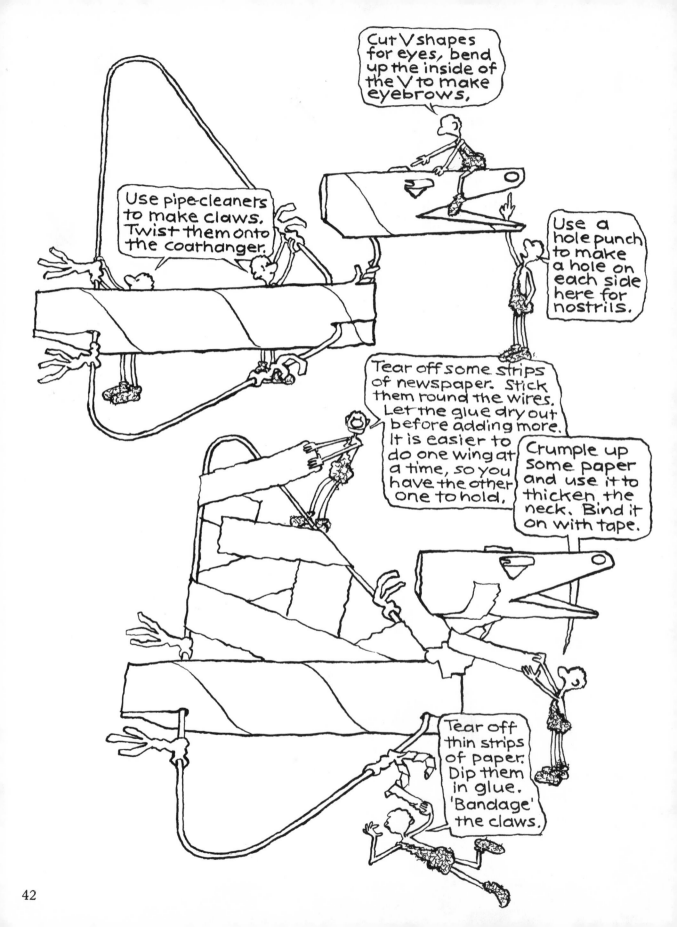

Cover the whole model with strips of gluey newspaper. Fold some over the leading edges of the wings. Let them extend beyond the trailing edge. Cover both the top and underside.

Trim off this corner before you stick paper over it.

When the glue dries, trim the trailing edge of the wing to shape.

Make four loose rolls of gluey paper. Stick two of them in a V shape between each hand and the body. Paste strips of paper over them onto the wings.

This is what it will look like before you have painted it

ALLOSAUR

There were lots of other dinosaurs, more or less closely related to tyrannosaurus rex, some of which might have been even more dangerous because they were smaller and more agile.

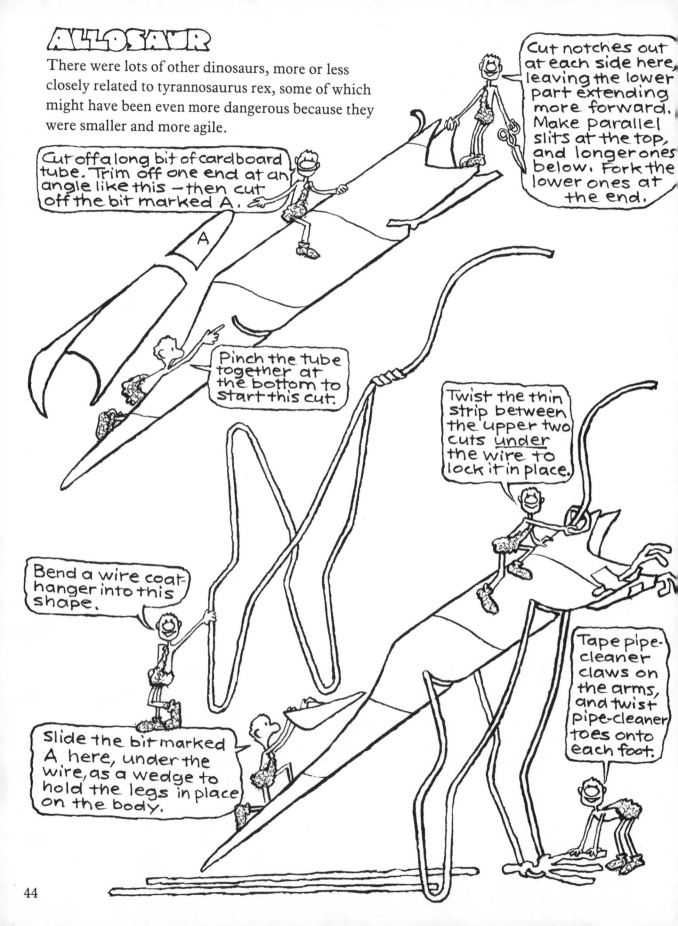

44

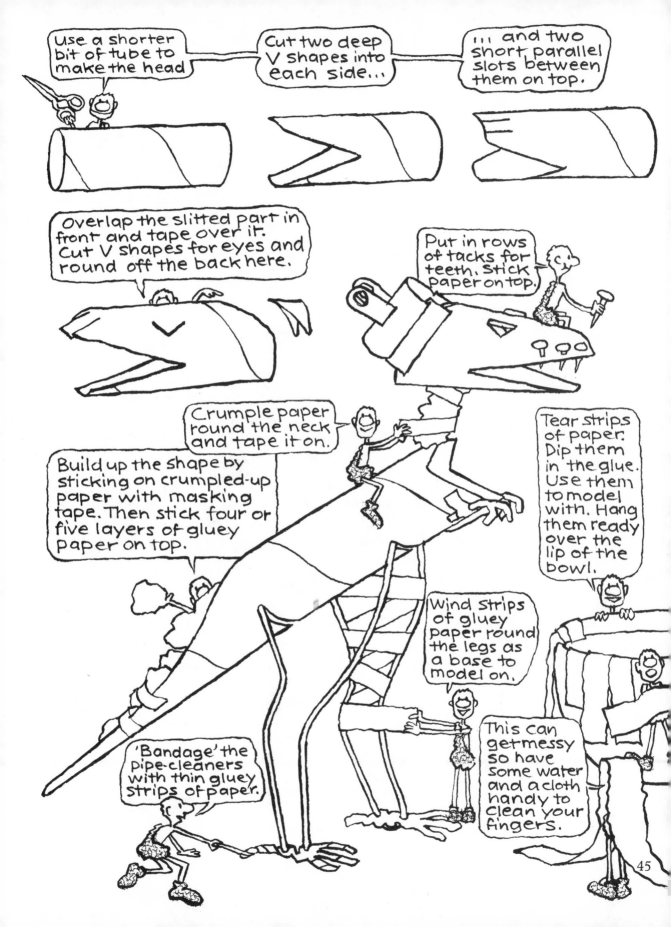

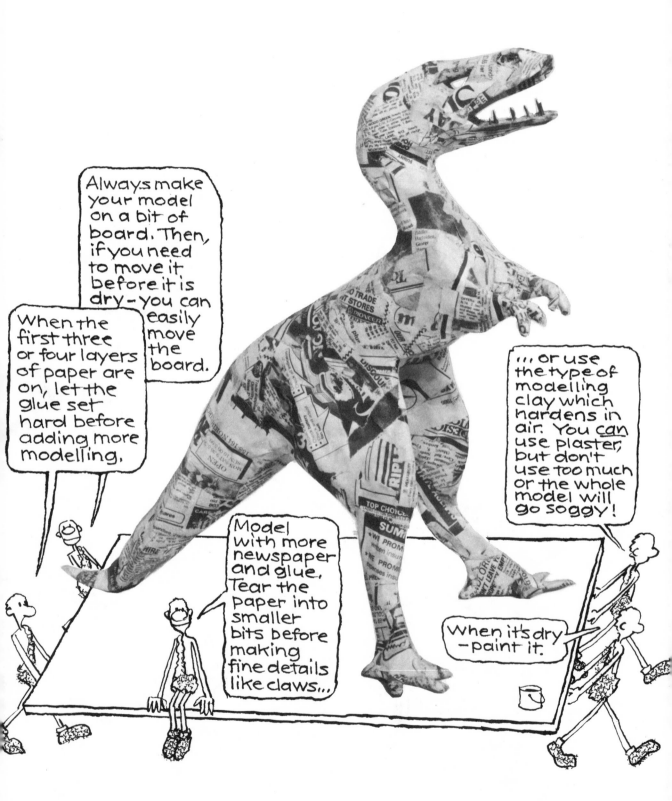

46

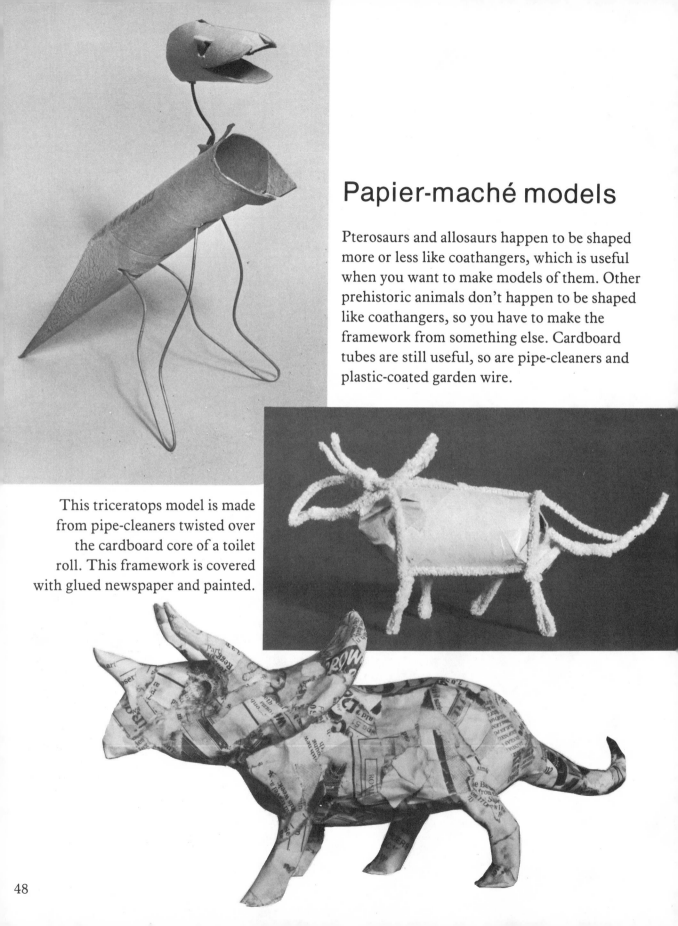

Papier-maché models

Pterosaurs and allosaurs happen to be shaped more or less like coathangers, which is useful when you want to make models of them. Other prehistoric animals don't happen to be shaped like coathangers, so you have to make the framework from something else. Cardboard tubes are still useful, so are pipe-cleaners and plastic-coated garden wire.

This triceratops model is made from pipe-cleaners twisted over the cardboard core of a toilet roll. This framework is covered with glued newspaper and painted.

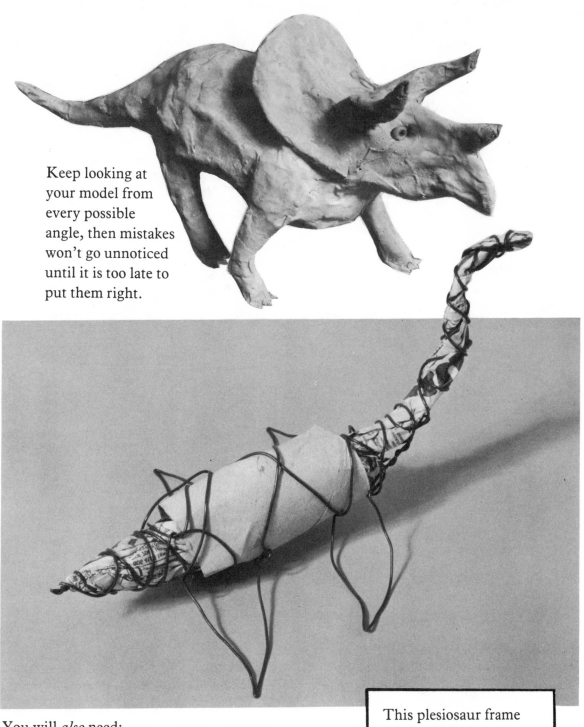

Keep looking at your model from every possible angle, then mistakes won't go unnoticed until it is too late to put them right.

You will *also* need:

Garden wire (plastic-coated) which comes in different weights from gardening shops and centres. Use heavy-duty garden wire for larger models. Bind it together with lighter wire or tape.

Tin snips or cutting pliers.

This plesiosaur frame is made from loosely rolled newspaper pushed through a toilet roll core, all wound round with garden wire.

Card models

Card is easier to fold accurately if you 'score' it first,
(run the blade of a *blunt* knife along the edge of a ruler where
you want to make the fold in the card).

You will need:
Some stiff white card or thin cardboard
Tracing paper
A sharp, hard pencil (H or HB)
A ruler
Scissors
A hole punch

Cut _____

Fold - - - - - - - -

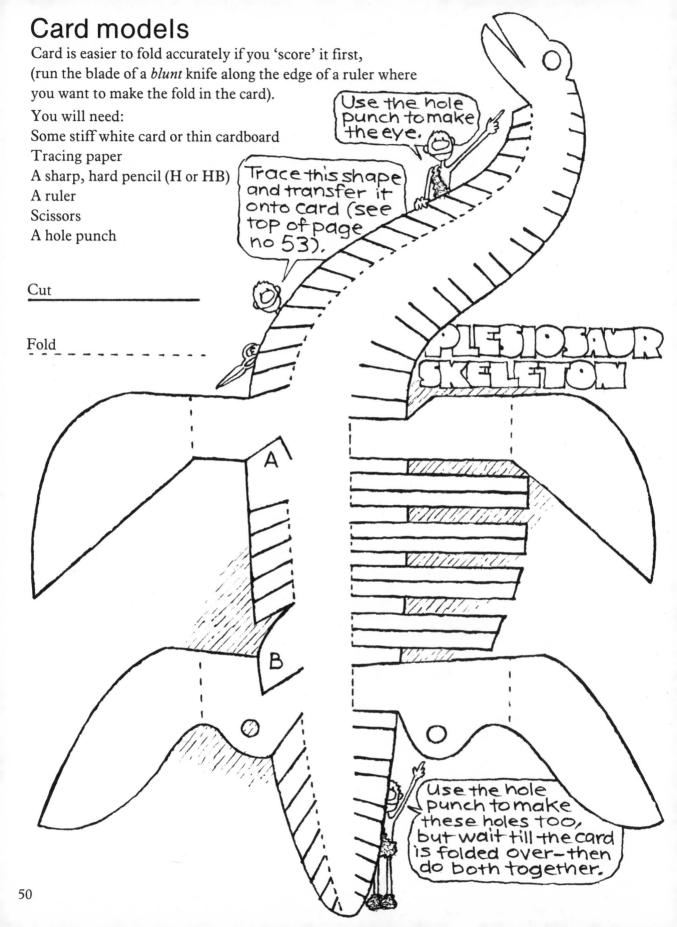

All that remains of the dinosaurs today is their fossilized bones and the occasional footprint. What we usually see in museums is reconstructed skeletons — but these make terrific subjects for modelling in themselves.

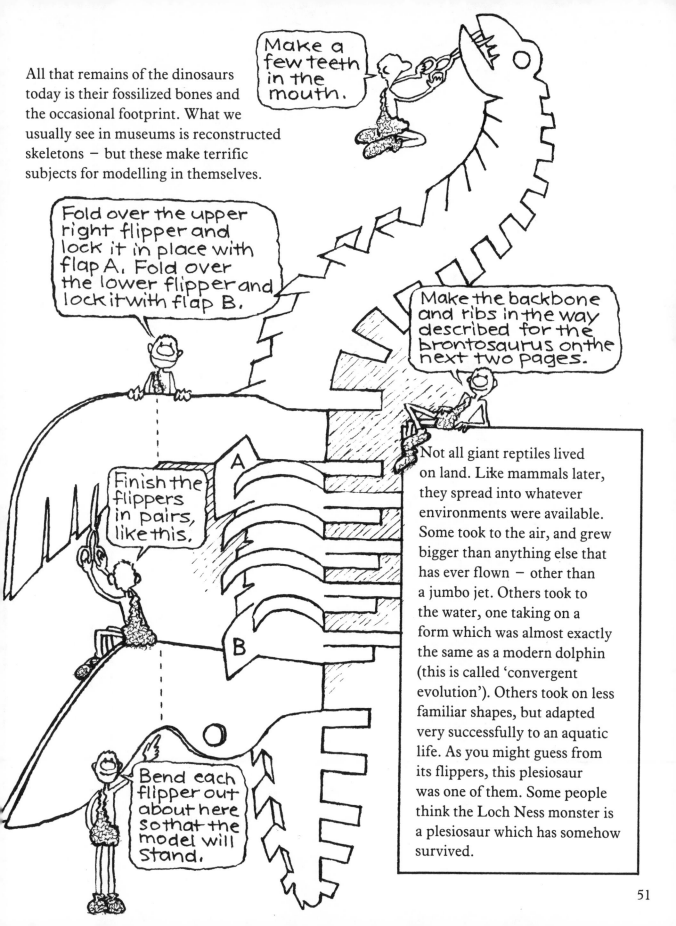

Not all giant reptiles lived on land. Like mammals later, they spread into whatever environments were available. Some took to the air, and grew bigger than anything else that has ever flown — other than a jumbo jet. Others took to the water, one taking on a form which was almost exactly the same as a modern dolphin (this is called 'convergent evolution'). Others took on less familiar shapes, but adapted very successfully to an aquatic life. As you might guess from its flippers, this plesiosaur was one of them. Some people think the Loch Ness monster is a plesiosaur which has somehow survived.

52

53

BACK LEGS

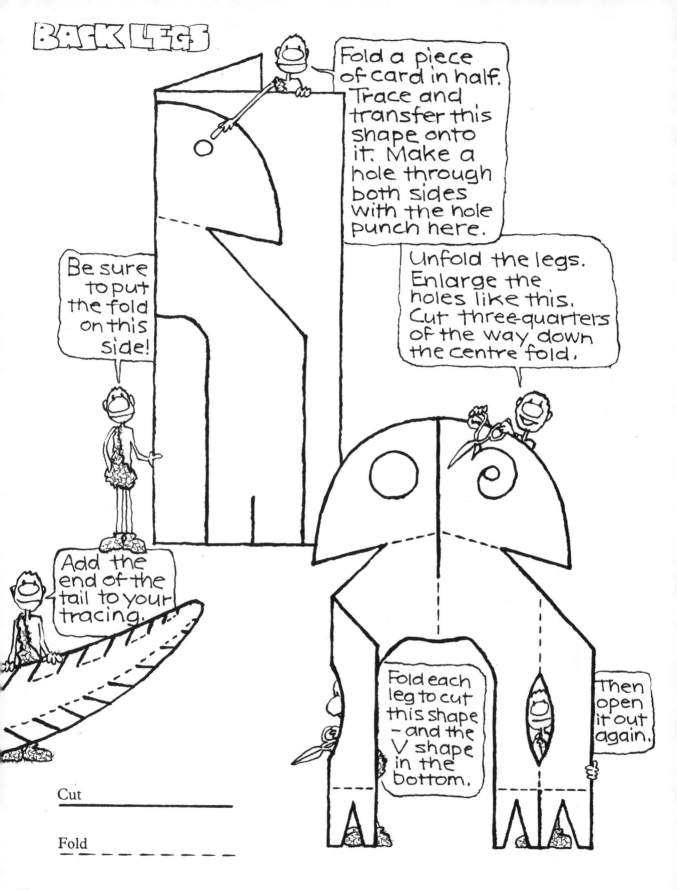

Fold a piece of card in half. Trace and transfer this shape onto it. Make a hole through both sides with the hole punch here.

Unfold the legs. Enlarge the holes like this. Cut three-quarters of the way down the centre fold.

Be sure to put the fold on this side!

Add the end of the tail to your tracing.

Fold each leg to cut this shape – and the V shape in the bottom.

Then open it out again.

Cut _____

Fold - - - - - - -

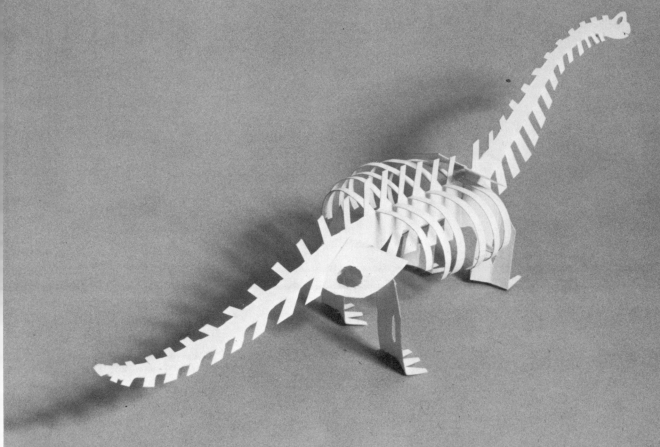

Paper models

Don't use thin, floppy paper unless you want thin, floppy models. Cartridge paper is best. It is much easier to fold paper accurately if you score it first. Don't try to force the folds – *persuade* them gently into place. It sometimes helps to half-fold three or four before completing any. You can get curves (such as ribs) started smoothly by rolling the strips round a pencil. Don't paint these models (except details). If you want them coloured, make them from coloured paper. You don't *have* to make models from a single piece of paper without glue – but it's very satisfying to be able to.

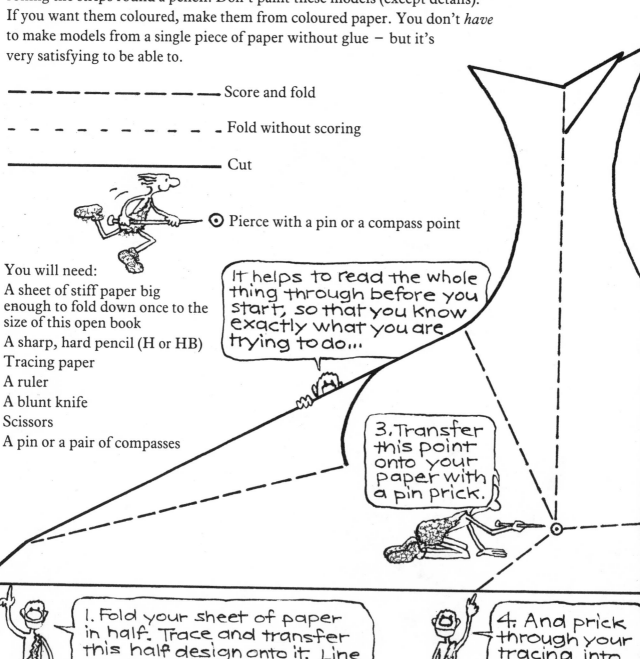

— — — — — — — — — Score and fold

- - - - - - - - - - Fold without scoring

————————————————— Cut

⊙ Pierce with a pin or a compass point

You will need:
A sheet of stiff paper big enough to fold down once to the size of this open book
A sharp, hard pencil (H or HB)
Tracing paper
A ruler
A blunt knife
Scissors
A pin or a pair of compasses

It helps to read the whole thing through before you start, so that you know exactly what you are trying to do...

3. Transfer this point onto your paper with a pin prick.

1. Fold your sheet of paper in half. Trace and transfer this half design onto it. Line up the bottom of the half design with the folded edge of the paper - but read the next instruction first!

4. And prick through your tracing into the paper at every point where lines meet. Then...

IGUANODON

Iguanodon was one of the first large fossils to be discovered. It was supposed that the bones were of a large lizard going, in life, on all fours like a modern iguana (hence the name).

A sharp, spiked bone they had left over they put on the nose, like a modern rhinoceros.

In fact iguanodon walked upright, like you, and the spikes (two of them) were on each of his hands like rigidly-extended thumbs. He was a vegetarian, but these built-in daggers must have made him a formidable opponent.

2. So that you don't have to trace over the fold (difficult), I've separated this pattern into two halves. Join up the halves in your tracing!

But he wouldn't have tried to pick a fight with the terrible tyrannosaurus rex – the largest land carnivore yet to evolve.

7. Cut out the shape and fold the model.

5. ...link the pin holes by scoring with the blunt knife on both halves of the folded paper.

6. Make the holes for the eyes and the nostrils with the hole punch through both layers of the folded paper. Then enlarge the eye-holes with scissors.

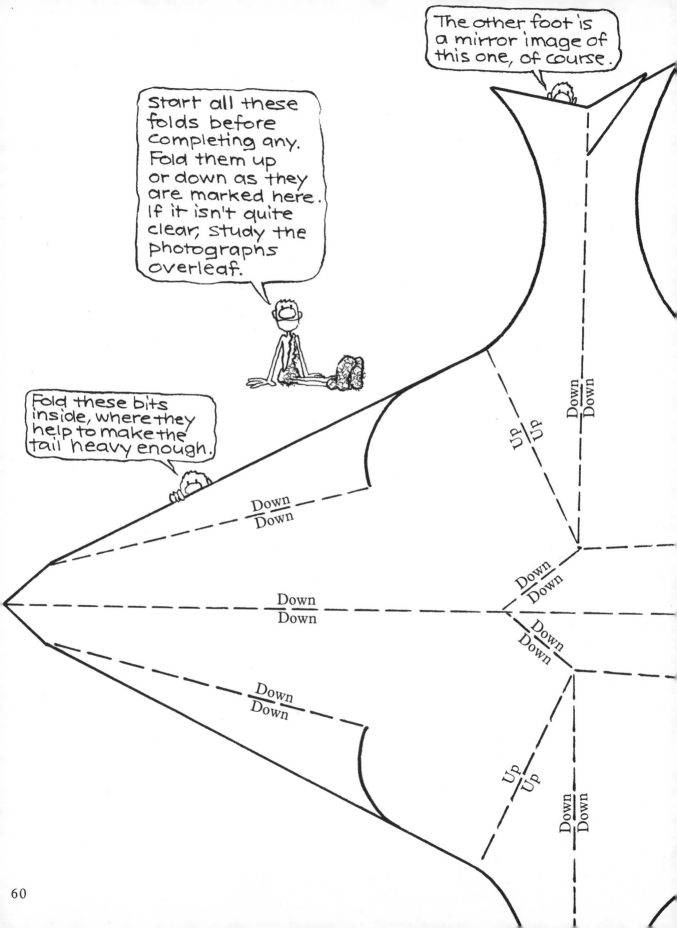

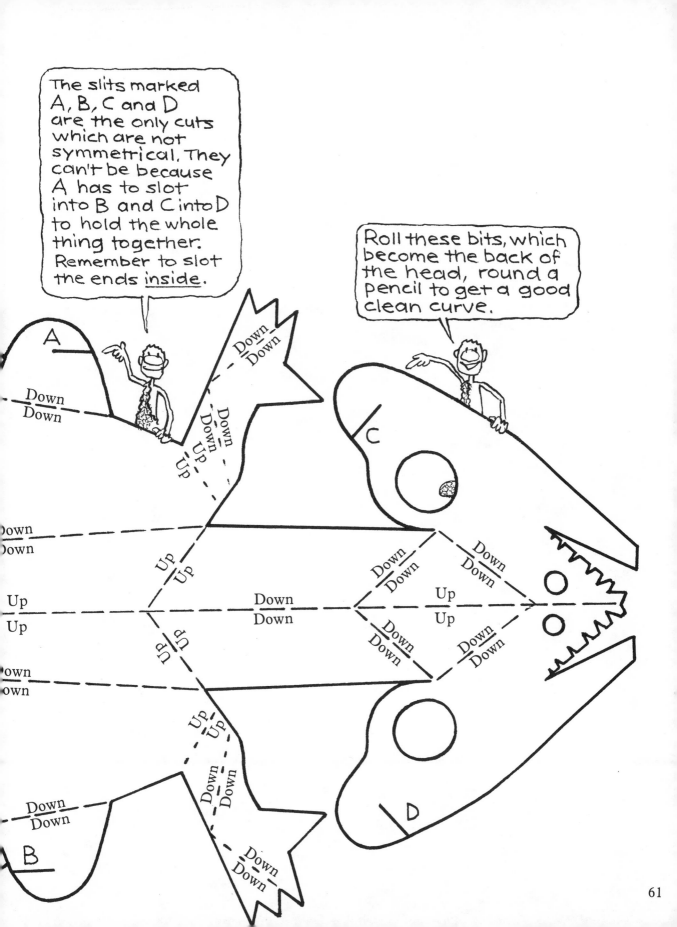

61

Below: The half-folded iguanodon. It can help to get all the folds started before completing any. Then ease them, don't force them, into place. Slot the tabs together behind the head and under the belly with the ends inside, not outside.

Opposite page: Two views of the completed model.

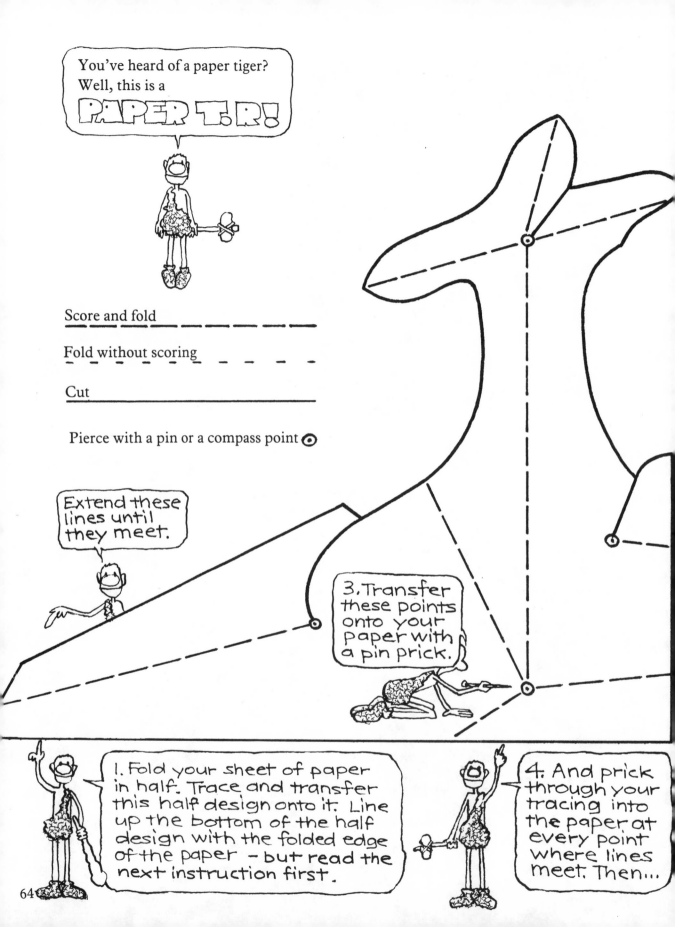

You've heard of a paper tiger?
Well, this is a

PAPER T. R!

Score and fold

Fold without scoring

Cut

Pierce with a pin or a compass point ⊙

Extend these lines until they meet.

3. Transfer these points onto your paper with a pin prick.

1. Fold your sheet of paper in half. Trace and transfer this half design onto it. Line up the bottom of the half design with the folded edge of the paper – but read the next instruction first.

4. And prick through your tracing into the paper at every point where lines meet. Then...

64

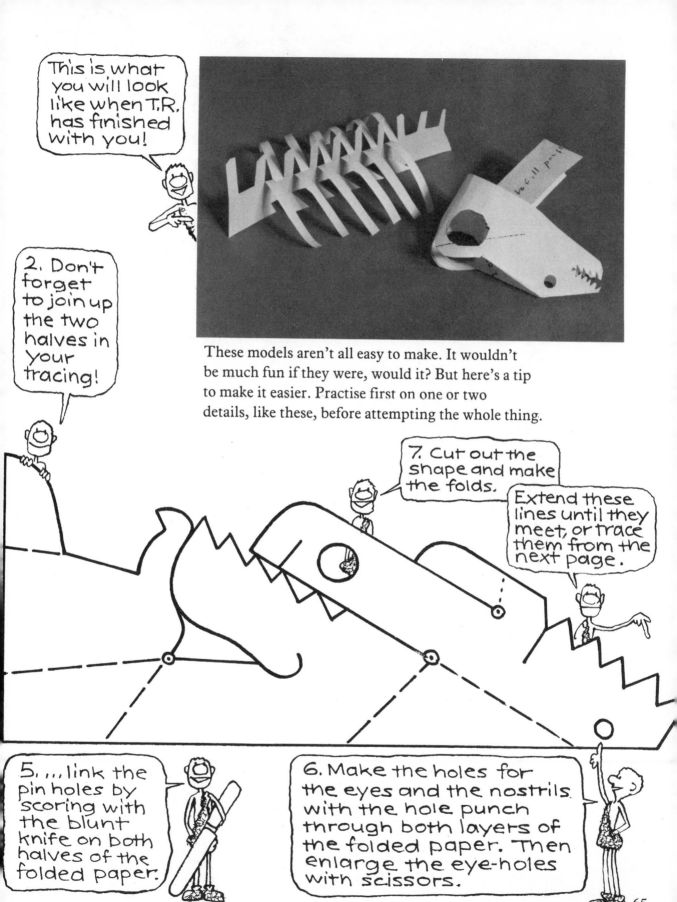

These models aren't all easy to make. It wouldn't be much fun if they were, would it? But here's a tip to make it easier. Practise first on one or two details, like these, before attempting the whole thing.

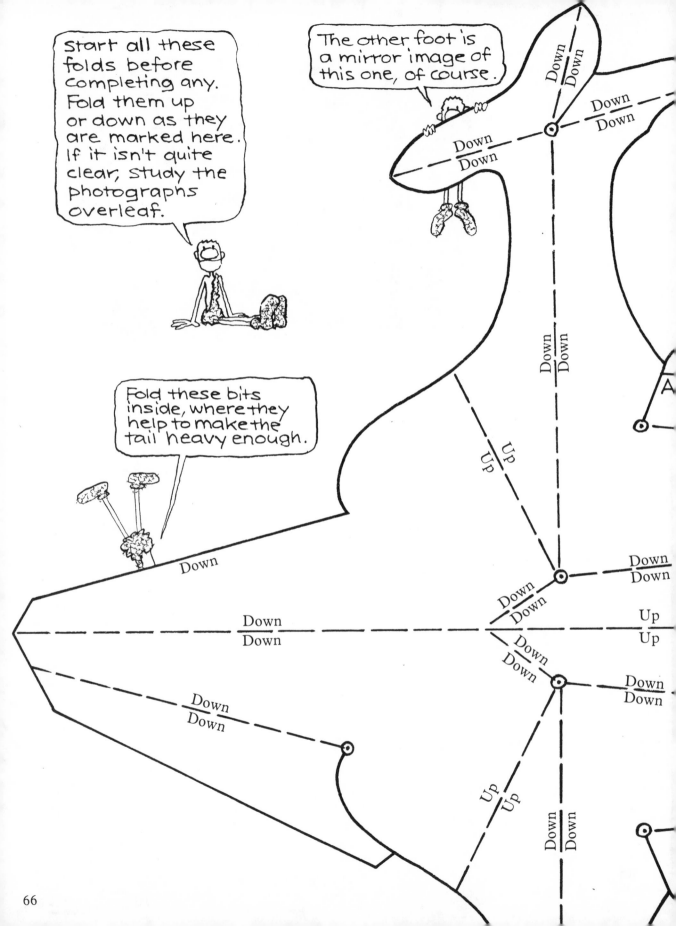

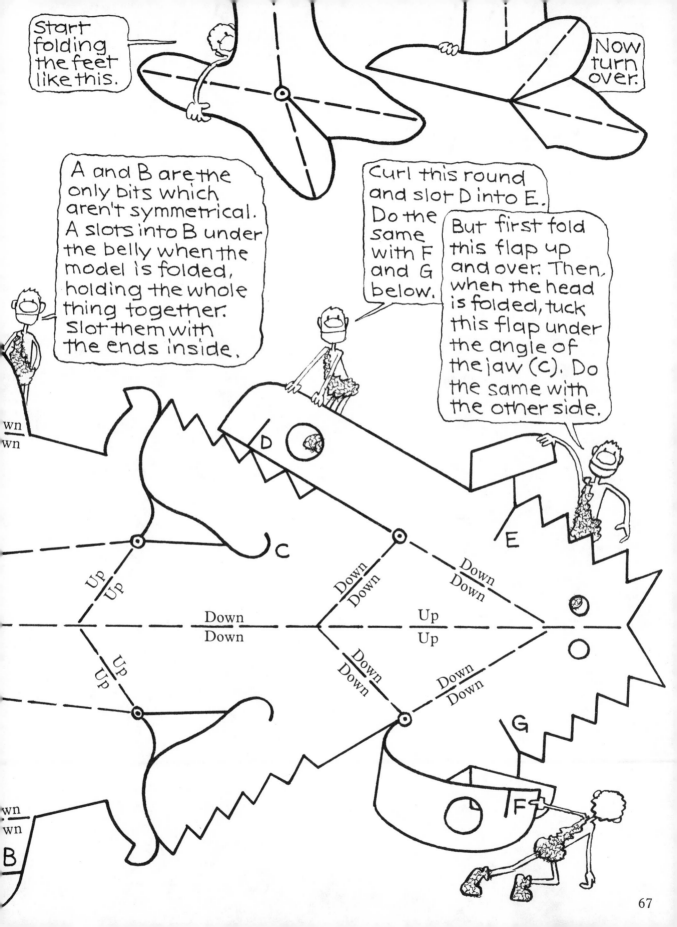

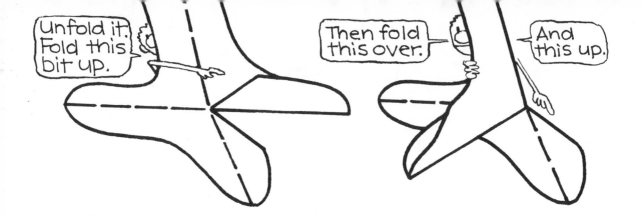

The half-folded model tyrannosaurus rex. As with the iguanodon,
it helps to get all the folds started before completing any. Remember, the
little tab which goes behind the angle of the lower jaw is effective
only if it is folded *out* (away from the head) and then down under the jaw.

Two views of the completed model.

PAPER MOSASAUR

There were lots of monsters of the deep, Son. Some much more fearful than the graceful, long-necked plesiosaur. This mosasaur looked a bit like a giant alligator, only with flippers instead of legs. He made JAWS look about as terrible as your average tadpole!

What's a mosasaur Grandpa?

You will need:

A sheet of stiff paper at least as big as this opened book

A ruler

A pencil (if you want to measure and mark where the cuts and folds should stop and start)

A blunt knife (for scoring)

Sharp scissors

Patience and care

Fold the sheet of paper in half longways. Keep the fold at the top. Press it flat.

Score two lines hard enough to mark both thicknesses, but _not_ so hard that you actually cut through the top one!

You can make these models stage by stage, as they are described. But it is a good idea to read to the end of each section before you start modelling, so that you understand the point of everything you do as you do it.

Make a cut here.

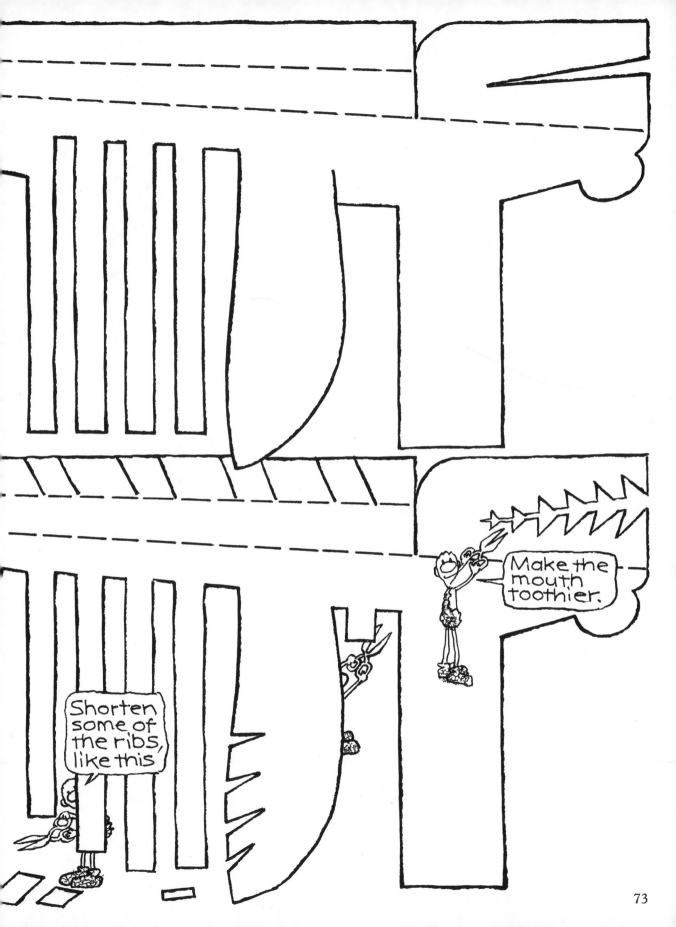

Now open it out flat to make the cuts which aren't the same on both sides.

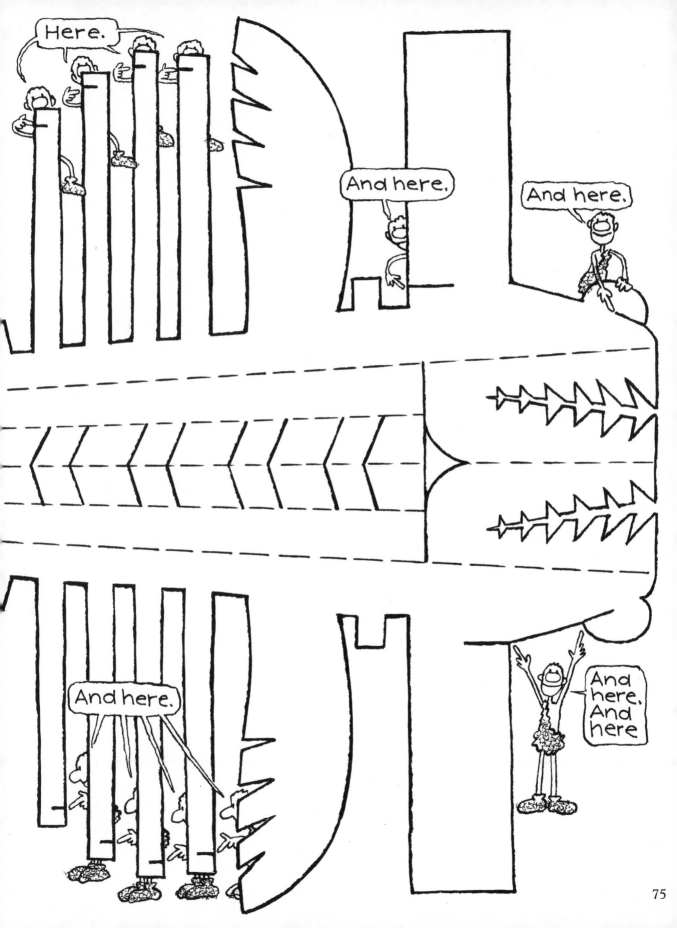

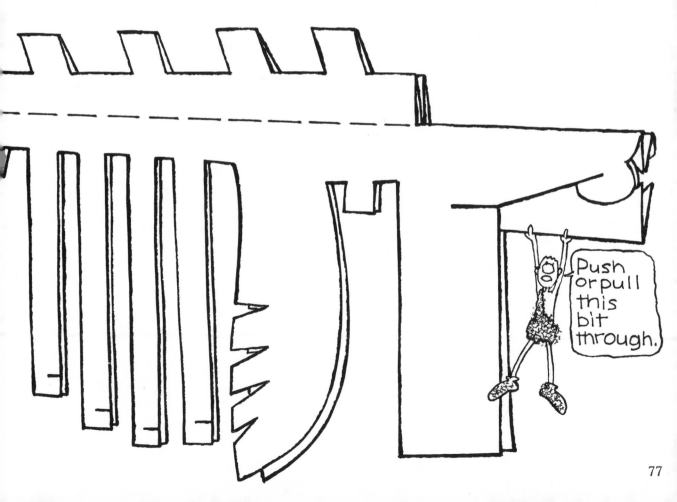

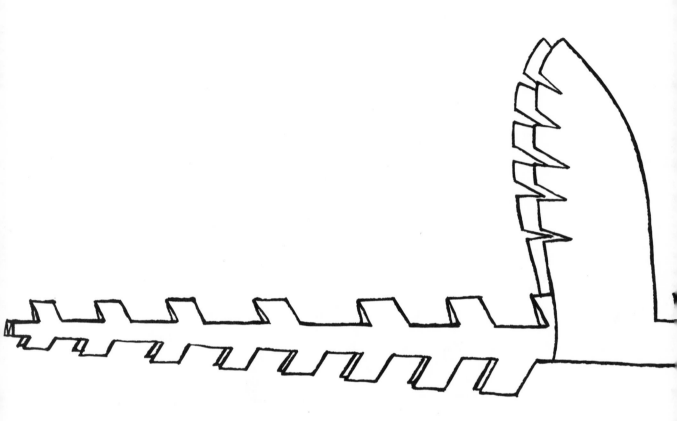

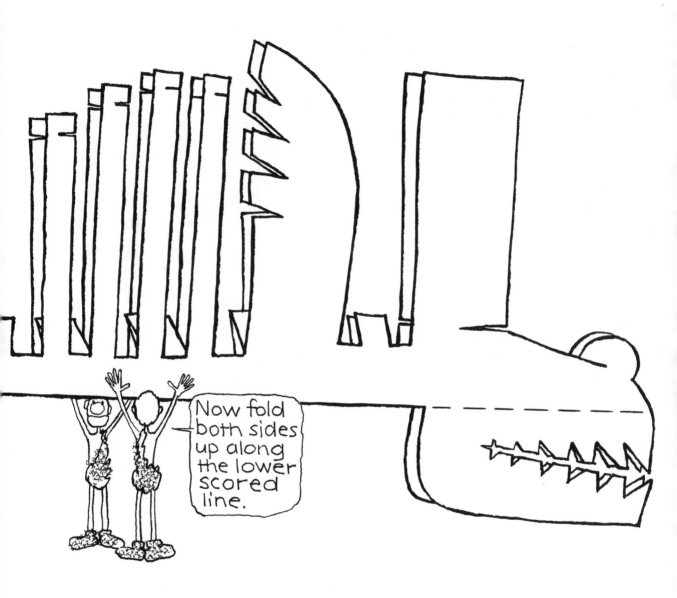

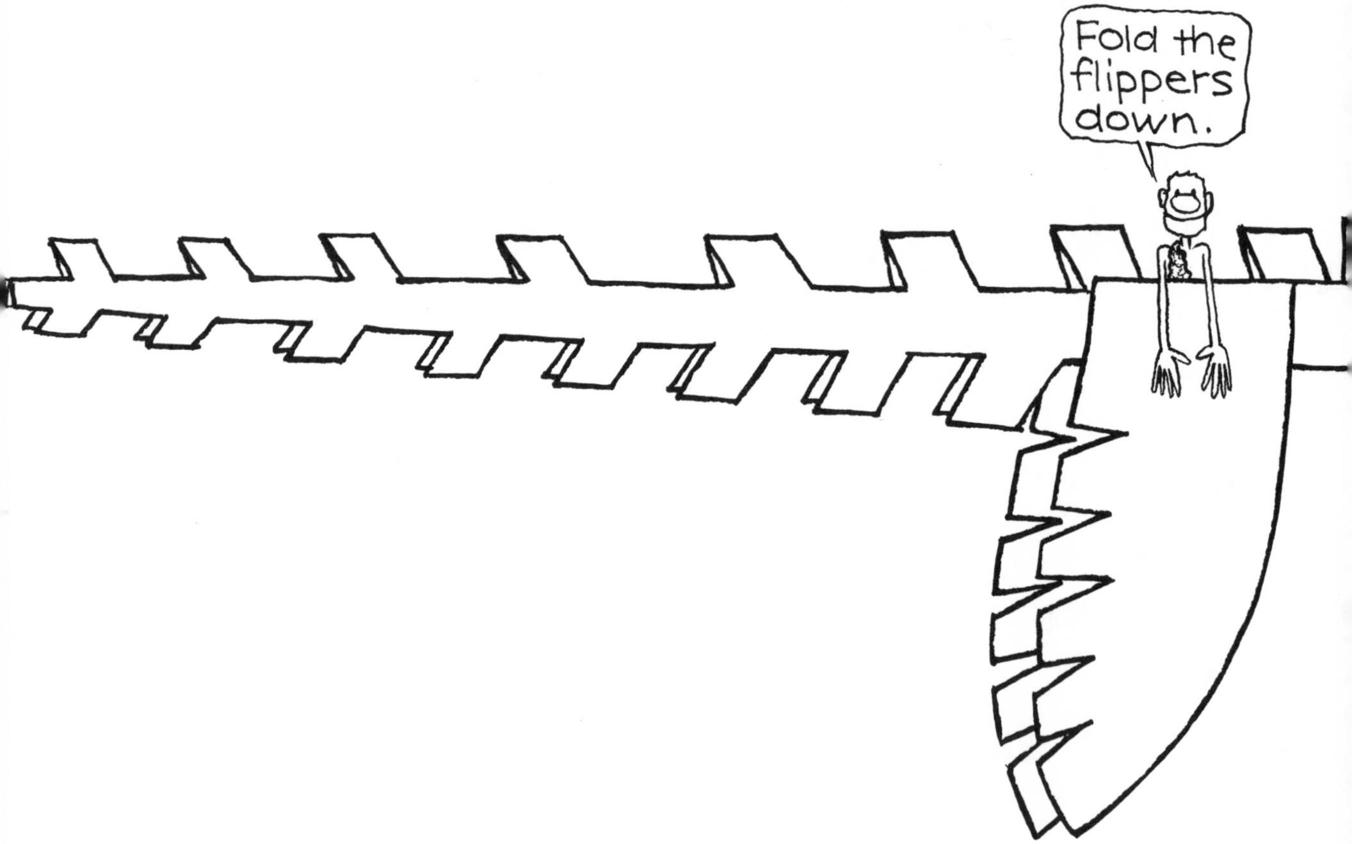
Fold the flippers down.

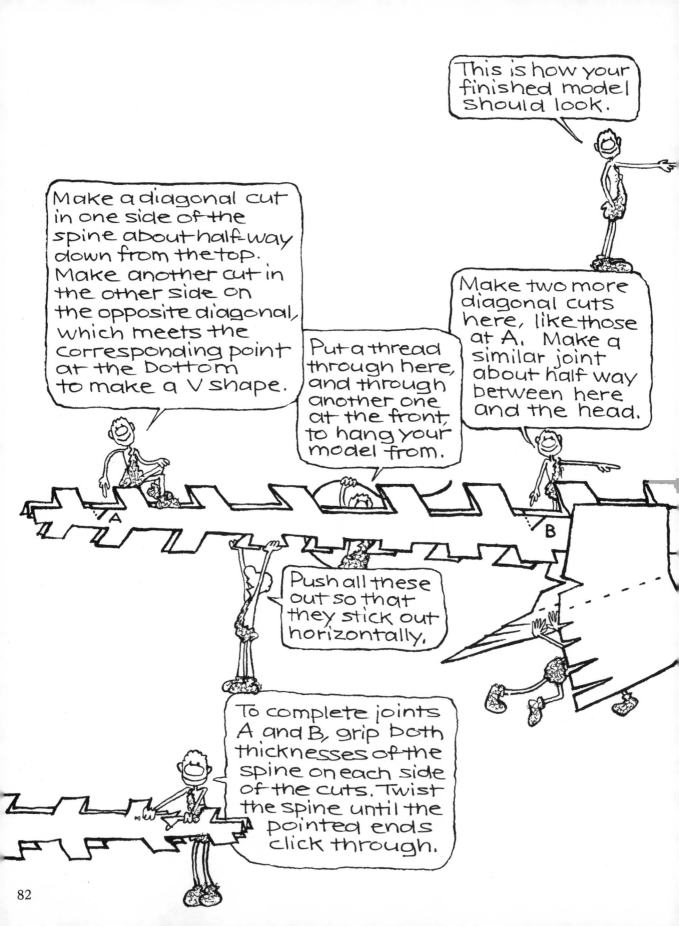

This is how your finished model should look.

Make a diagonal cut in one side of the spine about half-way down from the top. Make another cut in the other side on the opposite diagonal, which meets the corresponding point at the bottom to make a V shape.

Put a thread through here, and through another one at the front, to hang your model from.

Make two more diagonal cuts here, like those at A. Make a similar joint about half way between here and the head.

Push all these out so that they stick out horizontally.

To complete joints A and B, grip both thicknesses of the spine on each side of the cuts. Twist the spine until the pointed ends click through.

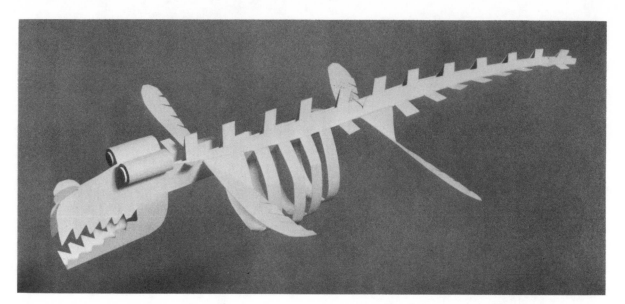

Roll down the strip on the other side too.

Press these tabs out horizontally on both sides.

Remove the pencil and tighten up the roll.

Curl each pair of ribs round and slot them together with the ends inside.

Fold all the flippers out at this angle. Don't score them first.

Phew!

Balsa-wood models

Cutting: Thicknesses of more than ¼ inch (6 mm) are usually easier to cut with a fretsaw and to trim to shape (if necessary) with a sharp craft knife. Thinner pieces may be easier to cut directly with the knife. Balsa wood is so soft that it crushes very easily. You need an especially sharp blade to make a clean cut. If used correctly, sharp blades are less dangerous than blunt ones. You don't have to press so hard, so they are less likely to slip and cause an accident. It is sometimes said that the most dangerous tool in any workshop is a screw-driver! BUT − knives that can cut wood can also cut fingers, so be very careful!

Never cut directly towards your other hand. Make sure the wood you are cutting is strongly held so that it won't slip. This means it has to be on a flat, non-slip surface. Make straight cuts against a metal ruler (the heavier the better). Don't try to cut right through in one go. Instead make a shallow cut first, carefully place the knife in the same cut and deepen it a little more with each successive cut until you are through. This will be especially necessary *across* the grain. An alternative to this is to make the first cut in the same way, which gives you a line to follow, then to make a series of little cuts right through the thickness, each one extending the cut further across the wood. This is the best method for cutting across narrow sections. If you are making such a cut against a ruler, support the end of the ruler on the sheet the section was cut from. This will help to hold it steady. If you want to round off an end, cut it off square first, then pare away the corners in a series of little cuts. If you haven't used balsa before, make some practise cuts in a spare piece before starting on a model.

Gluing: Thin bits with the grain running across them snap off very easily. The breaks are usually clean and can be 'invisibly' mended with P.V.A. glue. Even so, have the grain running *along* thin shapes as much as possible. This is easier to do because you can safely glue sheets of balsa with the grain at widely different angles (something you shouldn't do with other woods unless they are no thicker than veneers). It is a mistake to glue the end grain of any wood, *including* balsa. Note how, in order to avoid this problem, the spines on the back of the skeleton in this chapter are supported by the ribs and glued to them side grain to side grain.

You can use either P.V.A. (white) glue or balsa cement. P.V.A. allows you to slide one piece on another, to adjust its position, for a few minutes longer (which gives you the chance to get all four feet of a model flat on the ground, for example). It is also easier to clean P.V.A. off your fingers with a wet cloth.

Finishing: When the glue is set, finish shaping the model with the craft knife, files and glasspaper. Try to work *with* the grain, smoothing it down rather than roughing it up. The wood needs priming, to seal the surface, after which it can be painted with acrylic or oil based paints.

Alternative material: If you know how to use woodworking tools you could substitute plywood in different thicknesses for the balsa. Your models will be much more robust. You will have to drill holes for the eyes though (you can prod them through with a pencil point in balsa wood). You can stick plywood together with the grain at different angles too. That's how they make the stuff.

Why not ask your woodwork teacher if you can do it as a project?

You will need:

Tracing paper

A hard pencil (H, HB)

A soft pencil (3B – 6B)

A ruler

Scissors

A board or a bench to work on

A fretsaw

A craft knife (with renewable blades)

P.V.A. (white) glue *or* balsa cement

A bowl of water and some cloth (if you use P.V.A.)

A medium to fine round-section file

A medium to fine triangular-section file

A sheet or two of medium to fine glasspaper

Priming paint

Acrylic or oil-based paints

A brush

The appropriate solvent to clean the brush

Newspaper

BRACHIOSAUR

To make this one you will
need balsa wood in
the following thicknesses:
¼ inch (6 mm)
⅜ inch (9 mm)

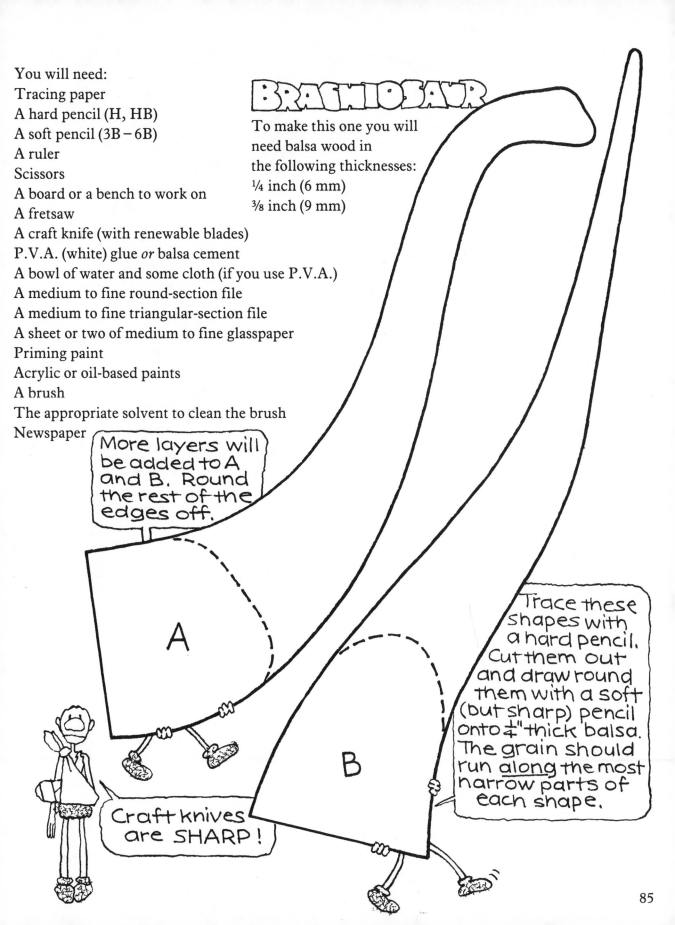

More layers will be added to A and B. Round the rest of the edges off.

Trace these shapes with a hard pencil. Cut them out and draw round them with a soft (but sharp) pencil onto ¼" thick balsa. The grain should run <u>along</u> the most narrow parts of each shape.

Craft knives are SHARP!

A

B

DUCKBILLED DINOSAUR

This is the basic duckbilled-dinosaur model. Duckbilled dinosaurs developed a variety of strange crests and ridges on their heads, although some didn't have them. But one could be incorporated into this model to make it more interesting, if you like.

You will need the following thickness of balsa wood:
¼ inch (6 mm)

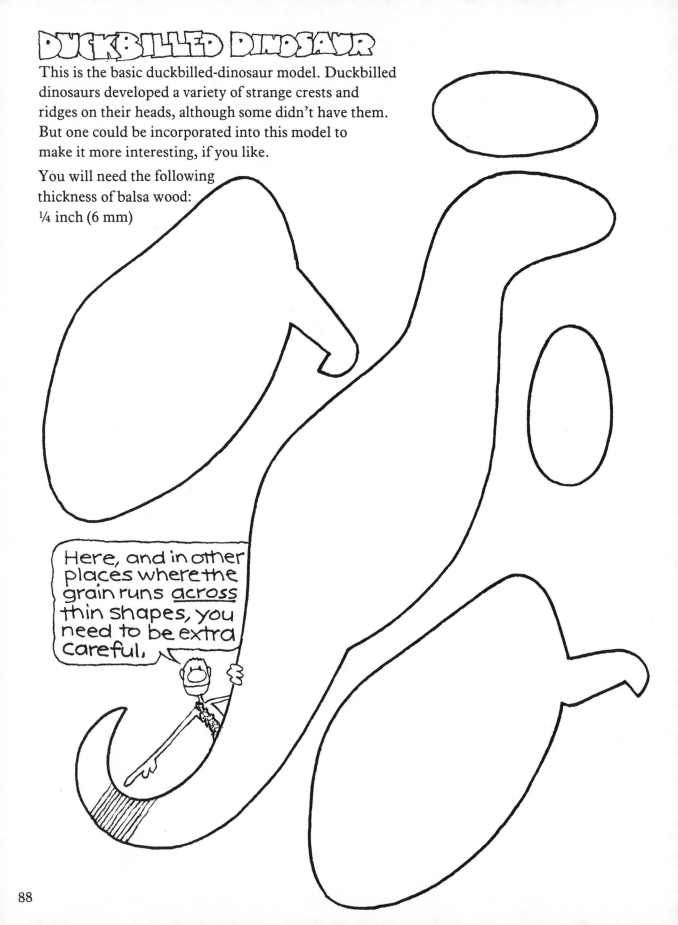

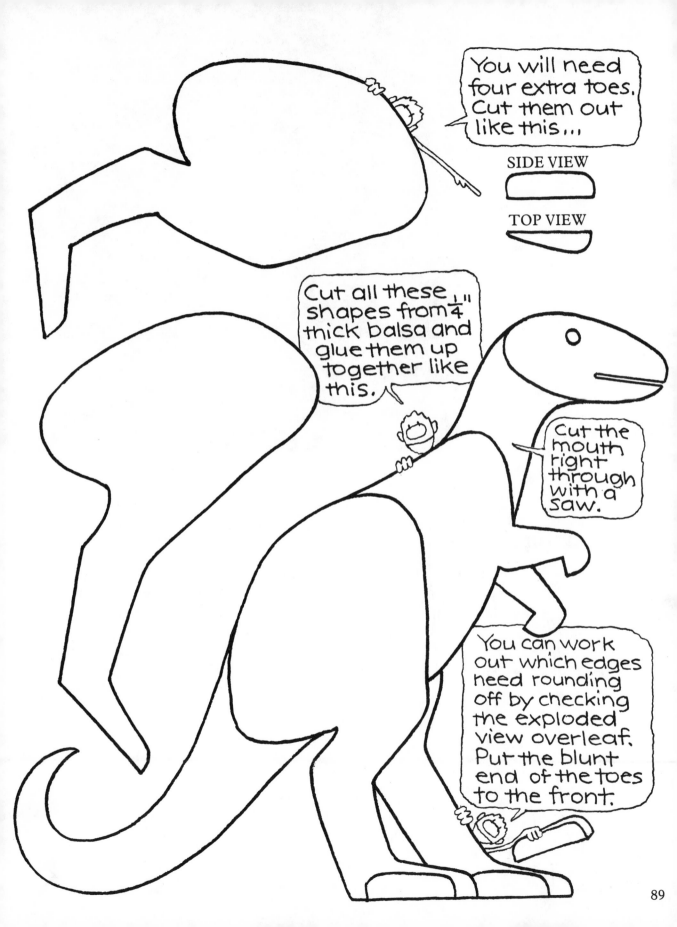

EXPLODED VIEW

Keep trying the parts together without any glue to check the fit, and that you are rounding off all the right bits and none of the wrong bits.

TRICERATOPS

You will need the
following thicknesses
of balsa wood:
½ inch (12 mm)
¼ inch (6 mm)

If you use ½" balsa-wood board for the centre of the model you can do some shaping in the width, like the tail here, which makes it look more alive.

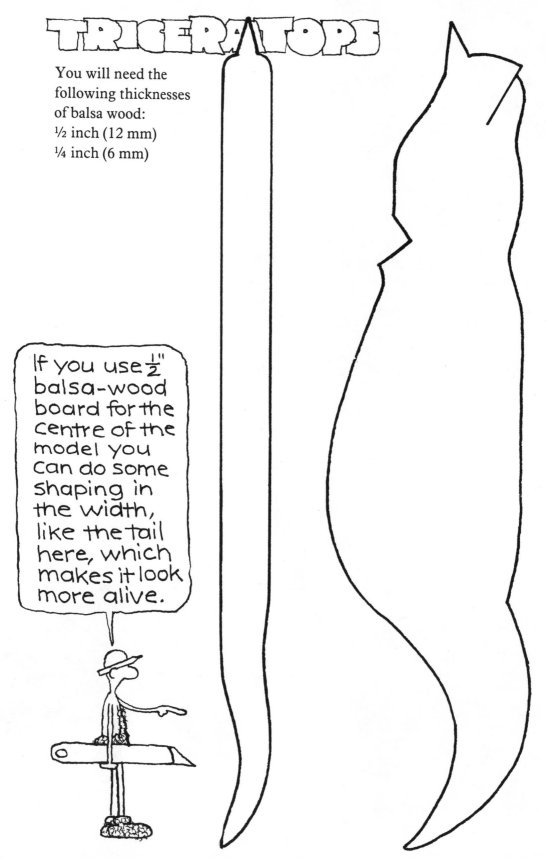

Horns (2)

Toes (8)

Cut all these shapes from $\frac{1}{4}$" board. Make two horns and eight toes.

DIMETRODON

You will need the following thicknesses
of balsa wood:
1/16 inch (1.5 mm)
1/4 inch (6 mm)
3/8 inch (9 mm)

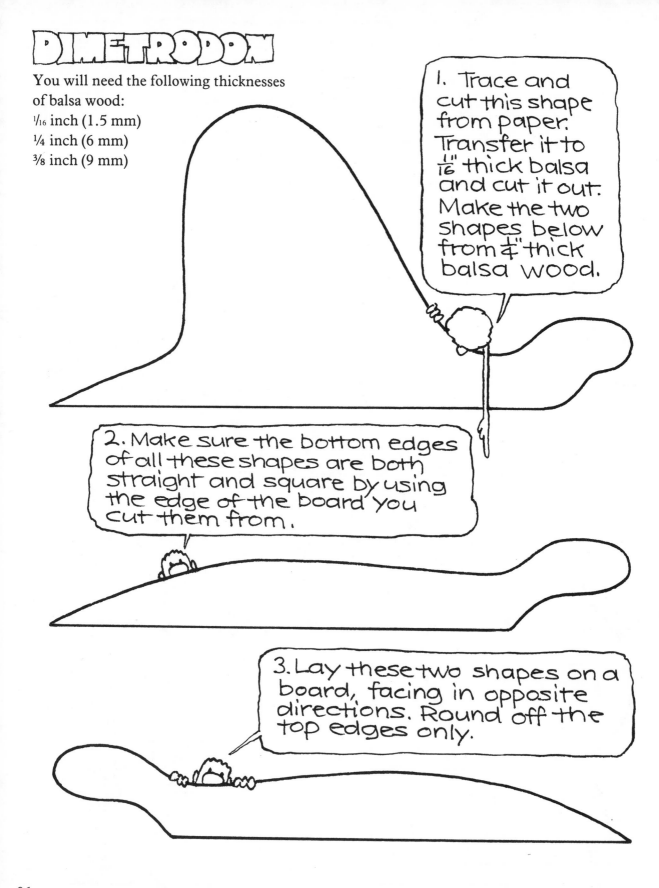

1. Trace and cut this shape from paper. Transfer it to 1/16" thick balsa and cut it out. Make the two shapes below from 1/4" thick balsa wood.

2. Make sure the bottom edges of all these shapes are both straight and square by using the edge of the board you cut them from.

3. Lay these two shapes on a board, facing in opposite directions. Round off the top edges only.

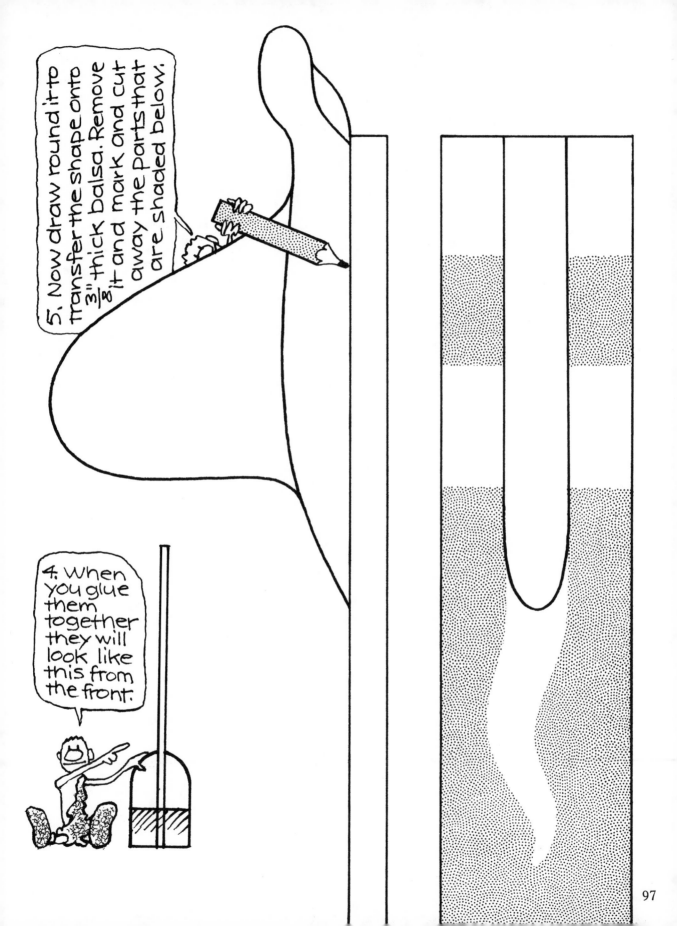

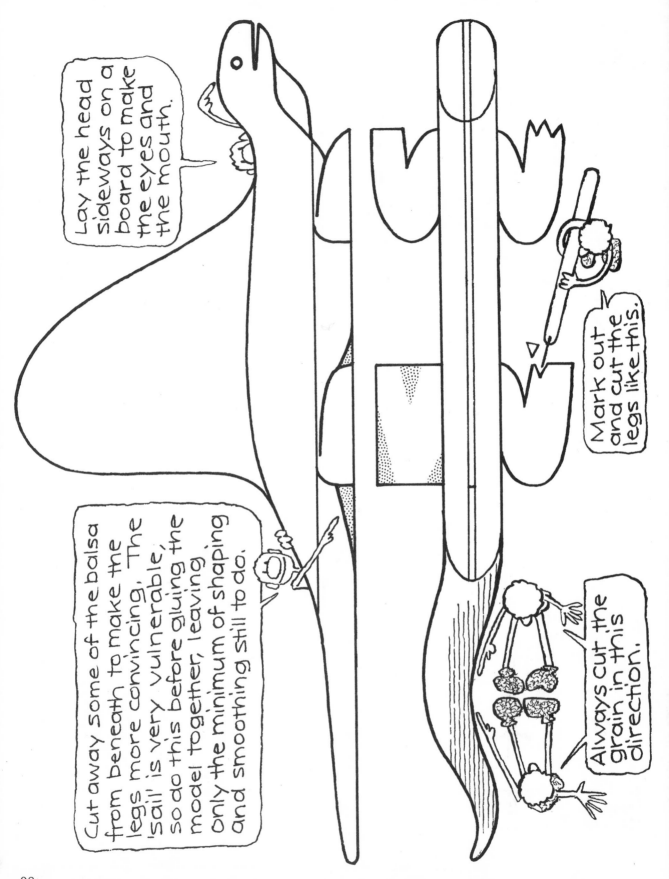

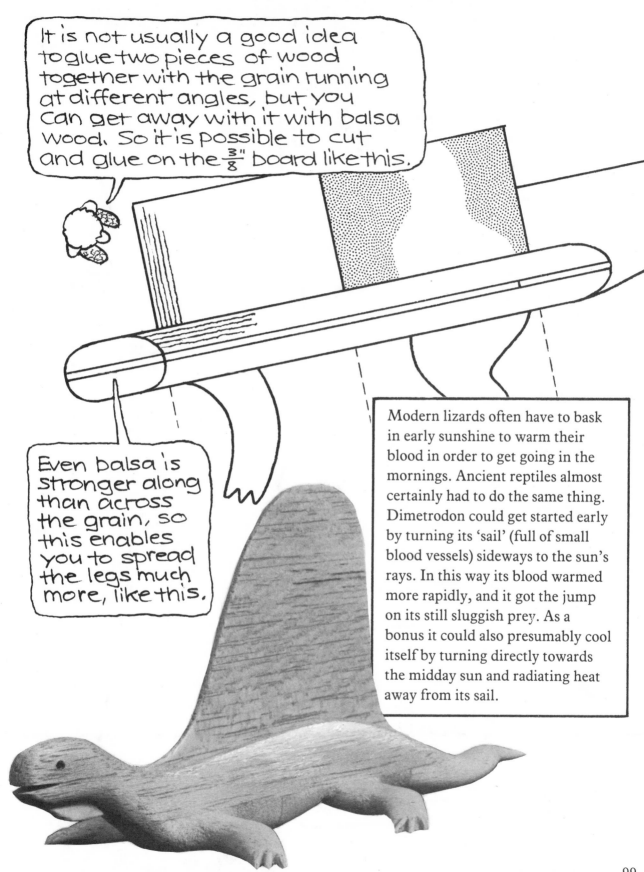

It is not usually a good idea to glue two pieces of wood together with the grain running at different angles, but you can get away with it with balsa wood. So it is possible to cut and glue on the $\frac{3}{8}$" board like this.

Even balsa is stronger along than across the grain, so this enables you to spread the legs much more, like this.

Modern lizards often have to bask in early sunshine to warm their blood in order to get going in the mornings. Ancient reptiles almost certainly had to do the same thing. Dimetrodon could get started early by turning its 'sail' (full of small blood vessels) sideways to the sun's rays. In this way its blood warmed more rapidly, and it got the jump on its still sluggish prey. As a bonus it could also presumably cool itself by turning directly towards the midday sun and radiating heat away from its sail.

PTEROSAUR

You will need the following thicknesses of balsa wood:

$1/16$ inch (1.5 mm)

$1/4$ inch (6 mm)

You will *also* need a length of triangular-section balsa wood $5/8$ inch (9 mm) on the widest side, and a needle and thread.

Pteranodons had the long thin wings of an expert glider. In some ways they must have looked very like the sail-planes and gliders that men fly today — only some of them were actually even bigger! They were pared down to the lowest possible weight, even losing their tails and teeth. This made the curious extension behind each pteranodon's head (at first thought to be for sexual display) a bit of a puzzle — until recent wind-tunnel tests proved the thing was like a weather vane, pulling the turned head back into the wind. It actually weighed less than the amount of muscle required to do the same job would have done!

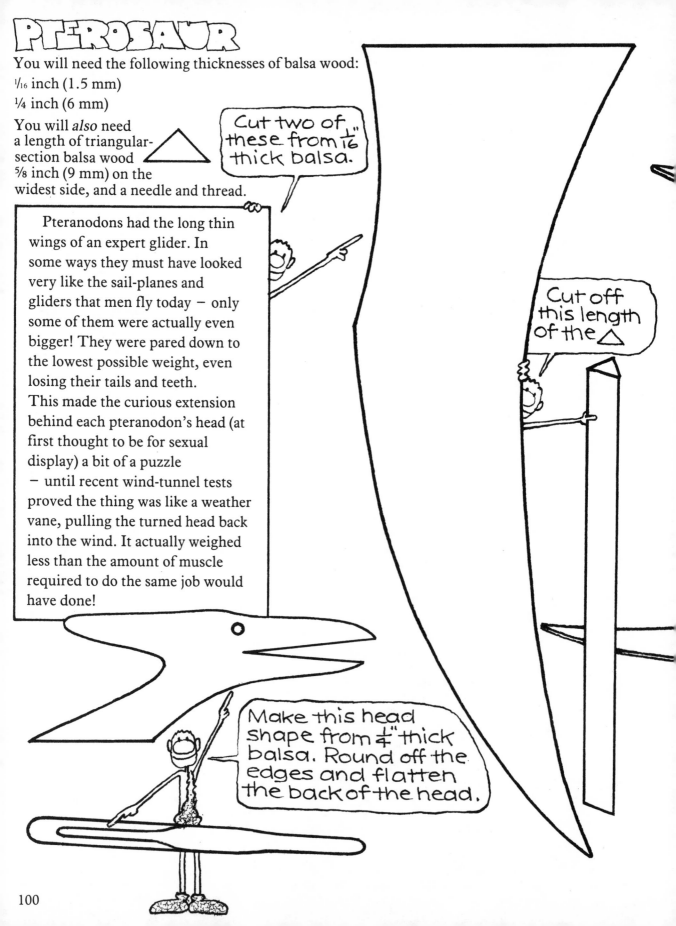

These animals must have flapped their wings occasionally, but probably less even than that great glider, the modern albatross, has to. They were much bigger than Albert Ross, the largest bird flying today. Instead of feathers, their wings, like a bat's, were flaps of skin stretching from finger tip to ankle. And two-thirds of their huge wings were supported only by the greatly extended bones of their little fingers!

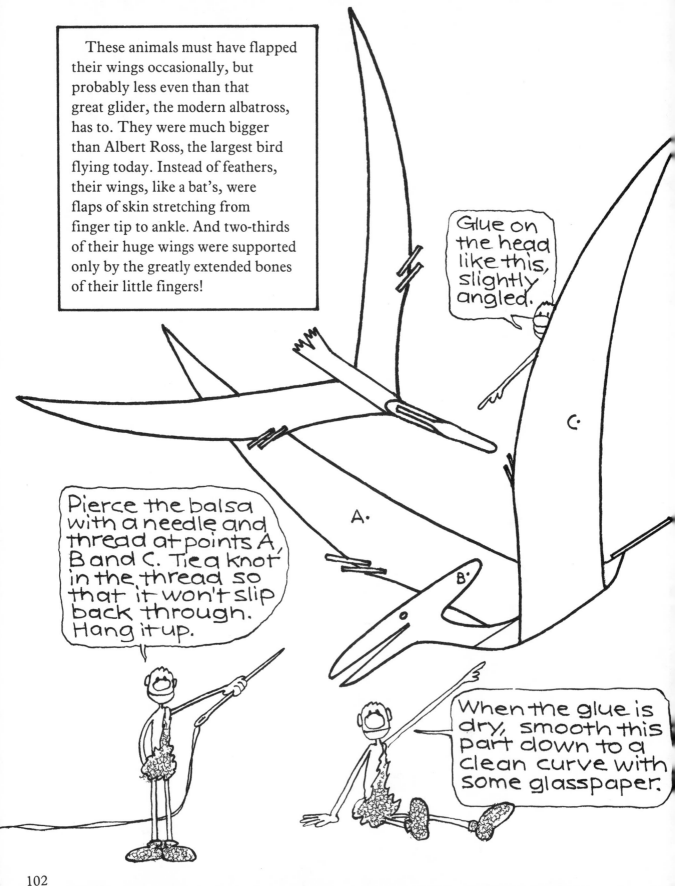

Glue on the head like this, slightly angled.

Pierce the balsa with a needle and thread at points A, B and C. Tie a knot in the thread so that it won't slip back through. Hang it up.

When the glue is dry, smooth this part down to a clean curve with some glasspaper.

PTEROSAUR MARK TWO

You will *also* need:
A wire coathanger
Wire-cutting pliers *or* tin snips.

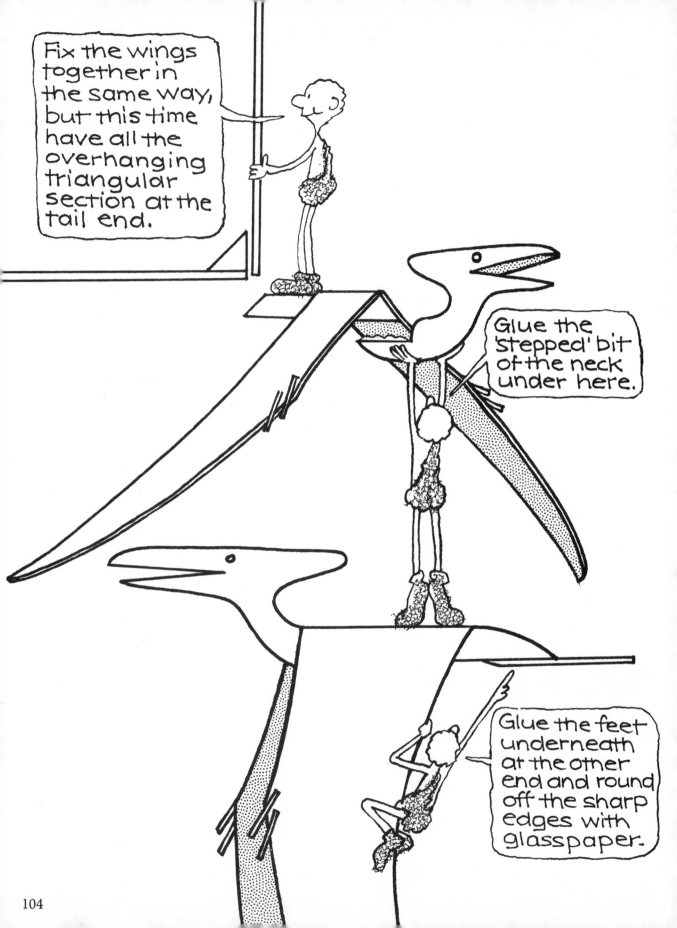

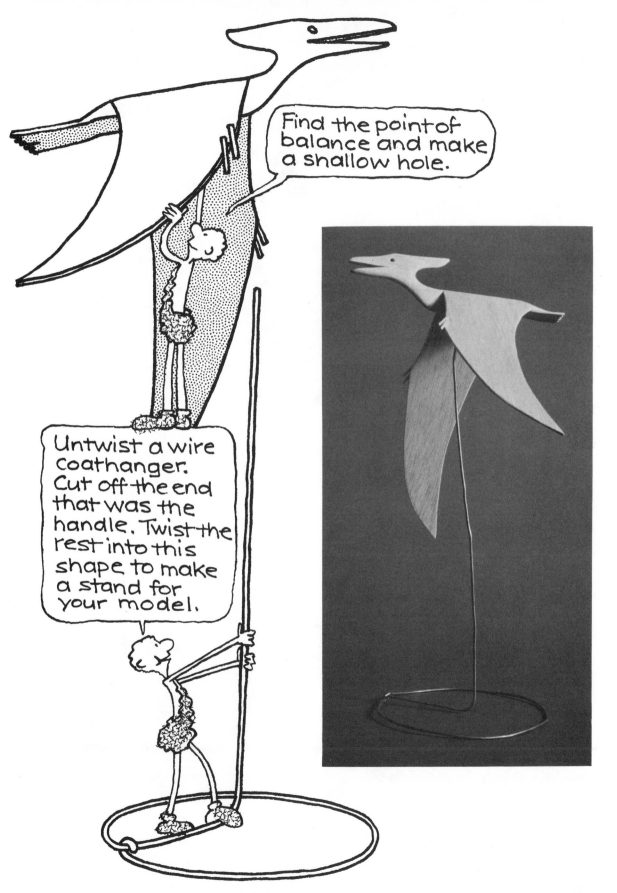

Find the point of balance and make a shallow hole.

Untwist a wire coathanger. Cut off the end that was the handle. Twist the rest into this shape to make a stand for your model.

A flock of pterosaurs will look very dramatic suspended from cotton threads. A threaded needle can easily be pushed through the balsa wood. Tie a knot in the cotton so that it won't slip back through the hole. Fix threads at a point about a third of the way down each wing and another at the back of the head.

The other models will make a good table-top zoo. Add a few carrot-top trees. Don't forget that the mammoth is about as remote from the time of the dinosaurs as you are!

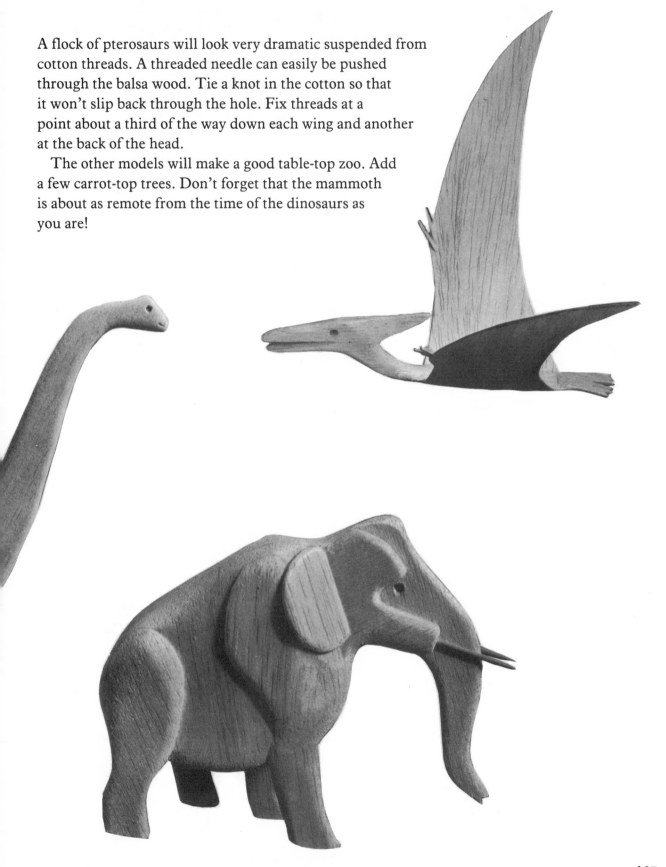

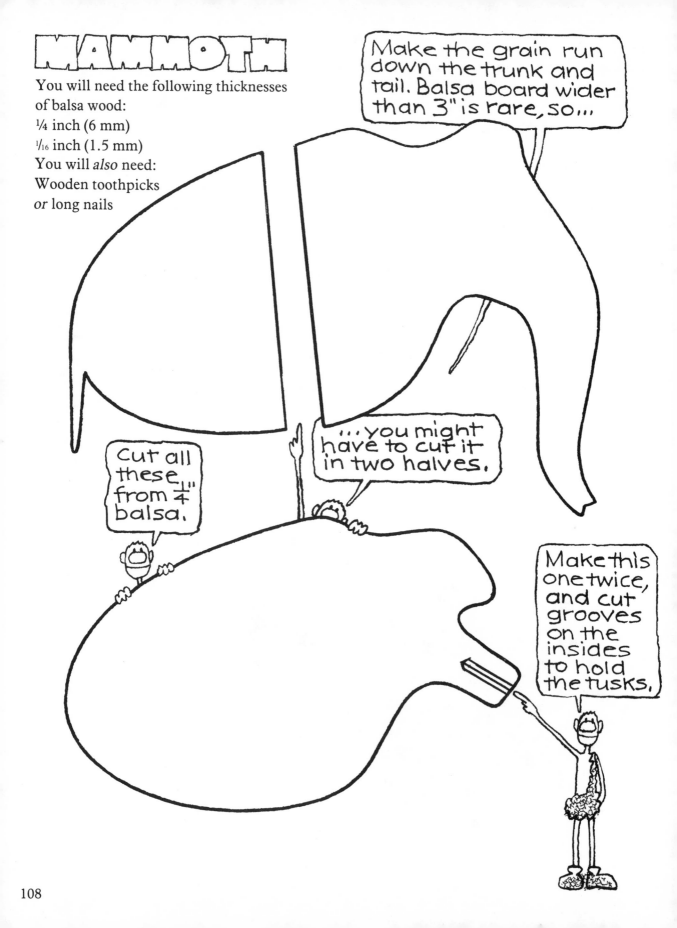

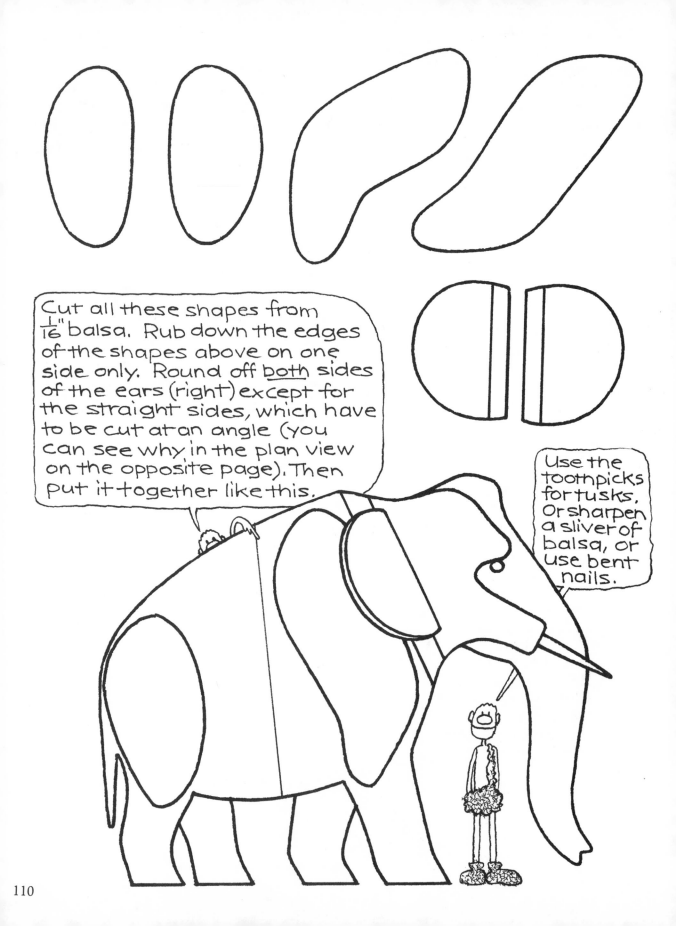

Cut all these shapes from $\frac{1}{16}$" balsa. Rub down the edges of the shapes above on one side only. Round off __both__ sides of the ears (right) except for the straight sides, which have to be cut at an angle (you can see why in the plan view on the opposite page). Then put it together like this.

Use the toothpicks for tusks, Or sharpen a sliver of balsa, or use bent nails.

Mammoths were closely related to modern elephants. They were hairy as an adaptation to the Ice Age (or perhaps their cousins are bald as an adaptation to a warmer climate). They had smaller ears to reduce heat loss, but their trunks were just as long, however cold it might have got. A trunk is as indispensable to an elephant as his right hand is to a man! Tusks are a sort of teeth, and don't have to keep warm. Mammoths' tusks were even longer and more curly than a modern elephant's. If you want your model to have long, curly tusks, use a couple of long, carefully-bent nails. Otherwise break a wooden toothpick and make your model a younger animal with straighter, shorter tusks.

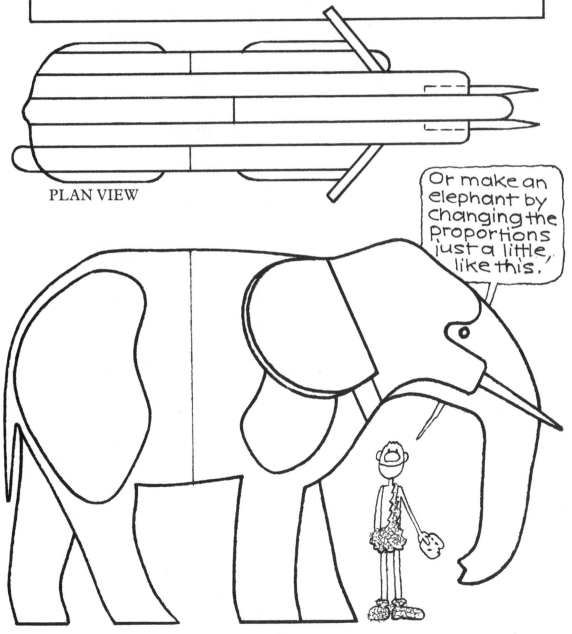

PLAN VIEW

Or make an elephant by changing the proportions just a little, like this.

BALSA-WOOD BRACHIOSAUR SKELETON

Balsa wood is also great for making skeletons. After you have made this one it should be easy to work out more designs from books and visits to museums.

For this one you will need:
¼ inch (6 mm)
⅛ inch (3 mm)

You will *also* need:
a length of triangular-section balsa wood
⅝ inch (9 mm) on the widest side.

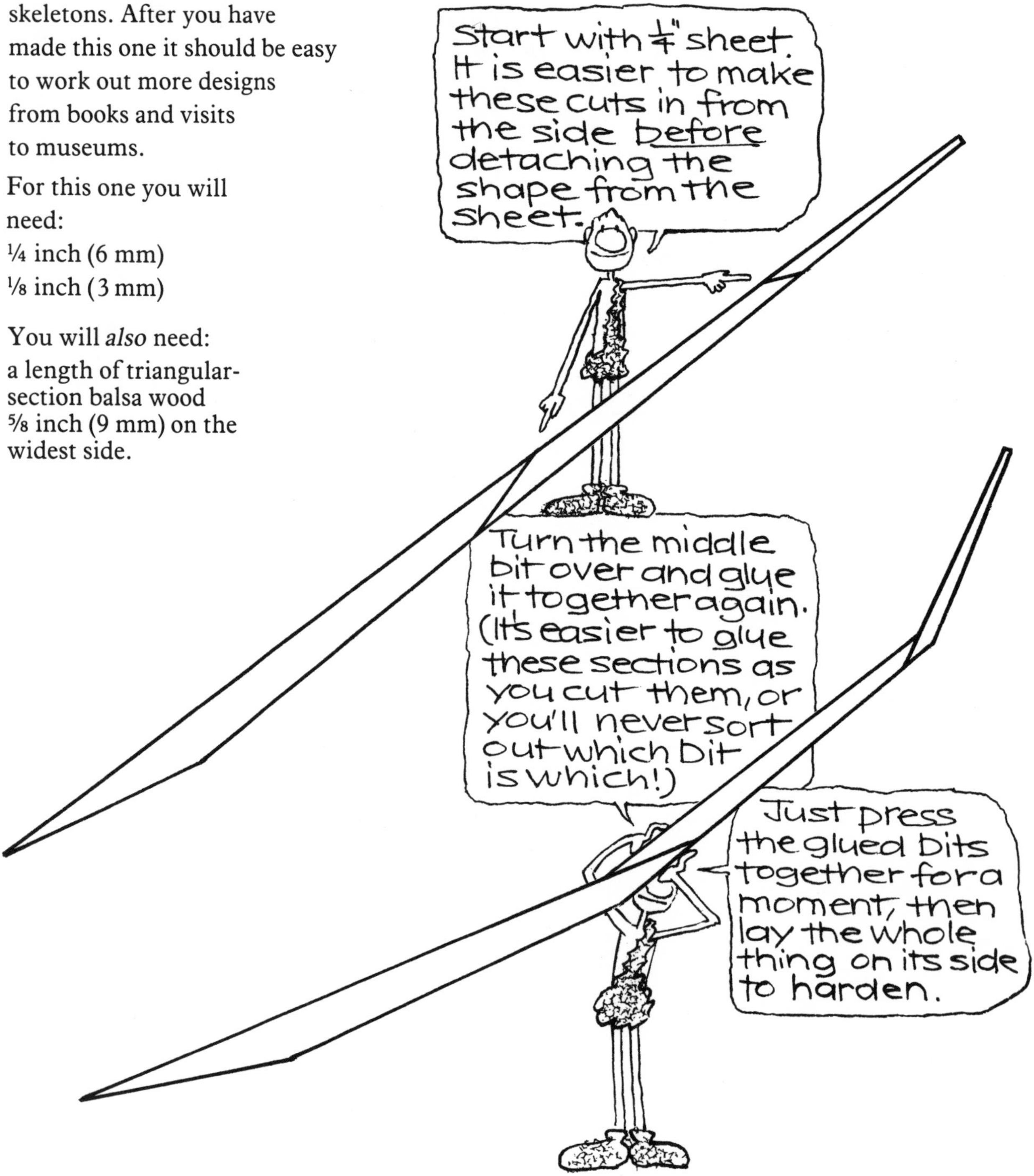

Start with ¼" sheet. It is easier to make these cuts in from the side *before* detaching the shape from the sheet.

Turn the middle bit over and glue it together again. (It's easier to glue these sections as you cut them, or you'll never sort out which bit is which!)

Just press the glued bits together for a moment, then lay the whole thing on its side to harden.

112

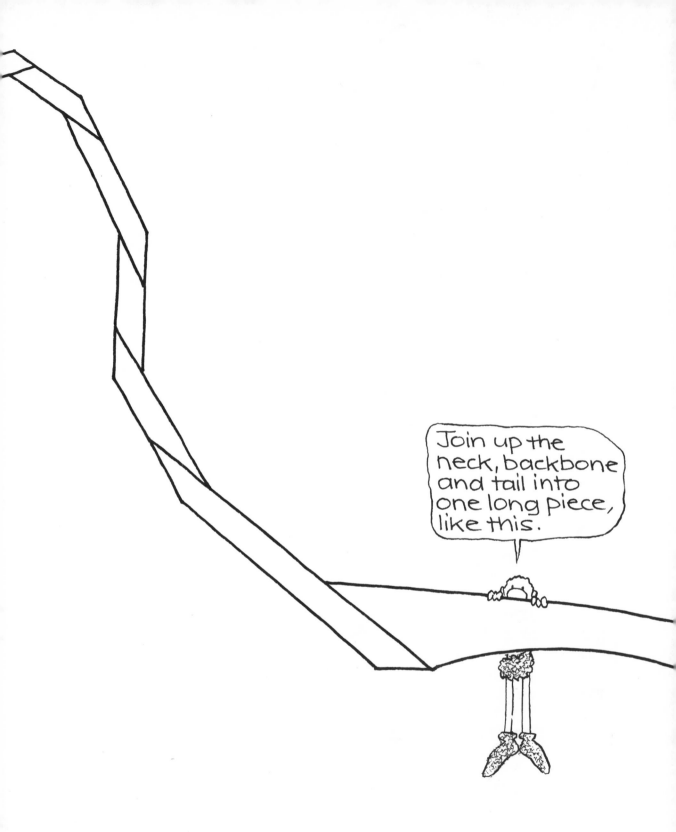

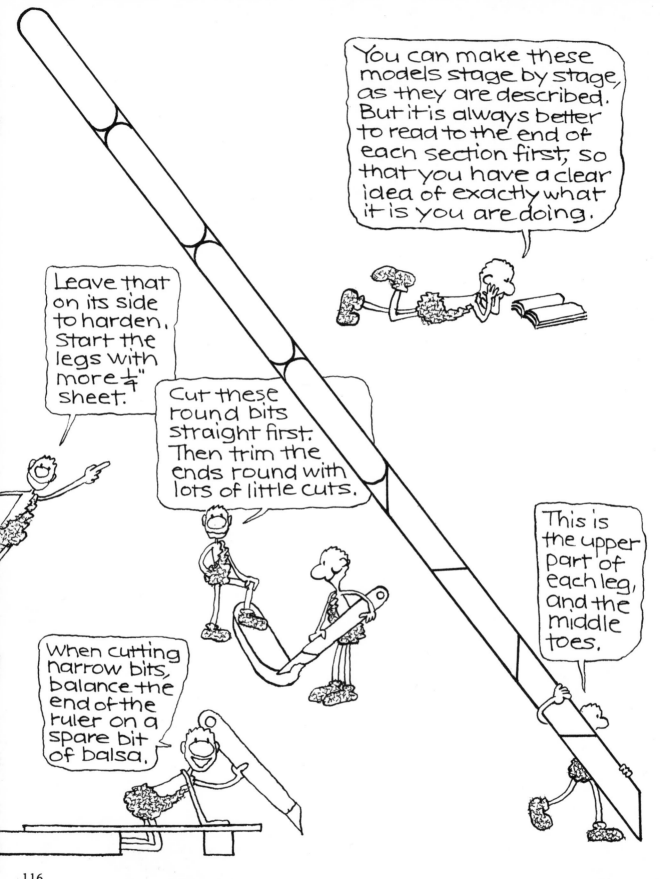

117

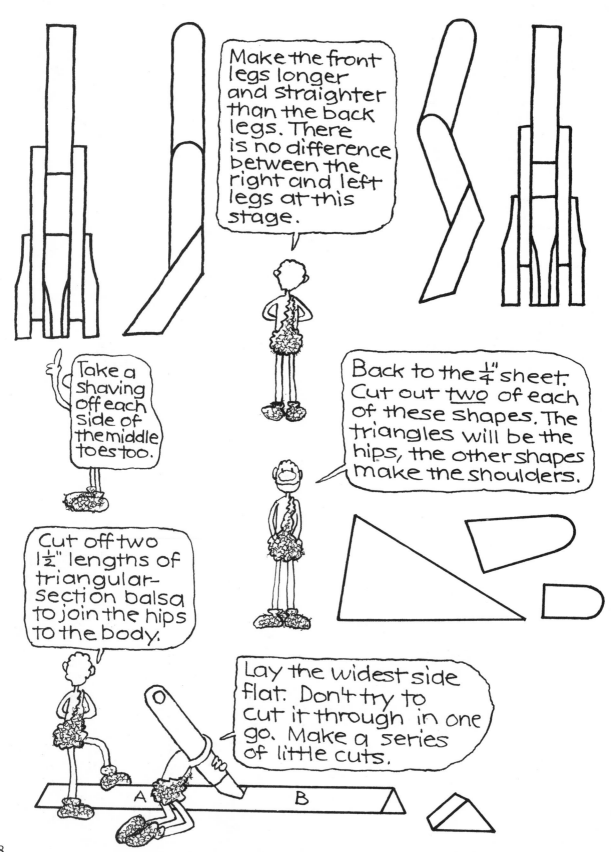

121

123

124

Overleaf: Two views of the balsa-wood brachiosaur skeleton model.

The rest of the spines fit between the tops of the pairs of ribs. If they won't go in easily, don't try to force them. You'll force the ribs off! Rub them down a bit and try again. When they slide in easily, glue them.

Stick these on top with one of the short sides glued. Put the side which slopes (the long side) towards the front.

Trim these triangles down a bit towards the end of the tail - above and below.

Stick these on underneath with the long sides glued.

125

Brachiosaurus was built along similar lines to a brontosaurus or a diplodocus. The differences were that its tail was shorter, it stood taller at the shoulders than the hips, it had its nostrils mounted right on top of its head and it might have been even bigger. Among its relations was the still larger supersaurus, ultrasaurus, larger yet, and breviparopus (they seem to have run out of superlatives) which was the biggest of the lot. Breviparopus was almost unbelievably large. It

could have weighed as much as a blue whale – or *twenty* large elephants! It seems to have reached a length of 157 feet (48 m)! If so it probably had the longest backbone ever evolved.

The idea that these animals must have lived in water is easy to sympathize with. Their huge size is easier to credit in an environment of water, and nostrils on top of the head are usually an aquatic feature. Some of them had hollow spaces in their bones, like birds. But one thing is sure – they didn't fly! Could these hollow bones have enabled them somehow to breathe *without* inflating their lungs while their bodies were submerged?

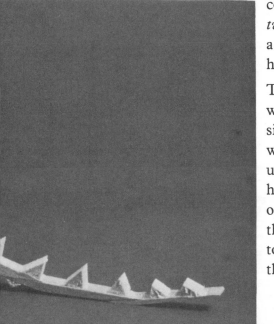

Models that work

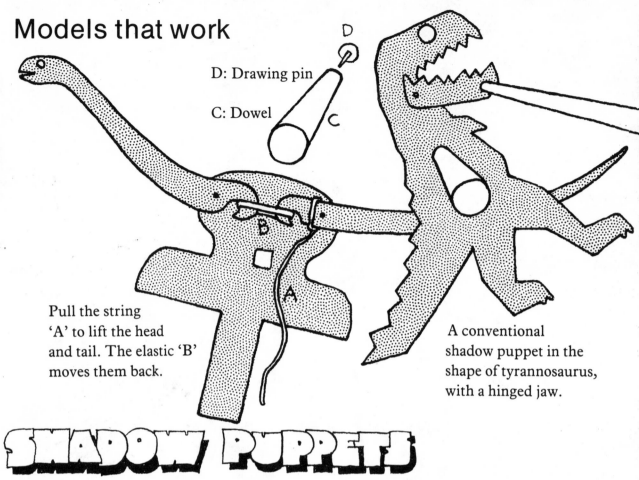

D: Drawing pin

C: Dowel

Pull the string 'A' to lift the head and tail. The elastic 'B' moves them back.

A conventional shadow puppet in the shape of tyrannosaurus, with a hinged jaw.

SHADOW PUPPETS

You need a cotton sheet or a big piece of white paper stretched over a frame, with a light placed behind it in a position to throw the shadow of the puppets (but not of the puppet handlers) onto this screen. The light must be covered so that it doesn't dazzle the audience. Light bulbs get *very* hot, so don't put the cover too close, and avoid having loops of flex all over the floor where they can get caught round people's feet.

The puppets can be made from black card and hinged by one of the methods shown. Small puppets can be held to the screen with drinking straws stuck on with sticky tape, large ones with dowels pushed onto a drawing pin through the card. Cut holes for eyes and tape red tissue over them.

You will need:
Stiff black paper or card
Scissors
Corks
Dowels

Drawing pins
Drinking straws
Sticky tape
Red tissue paper
A screen

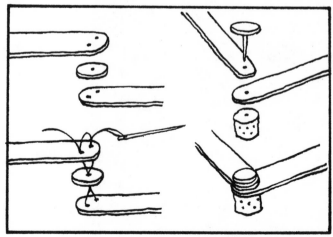

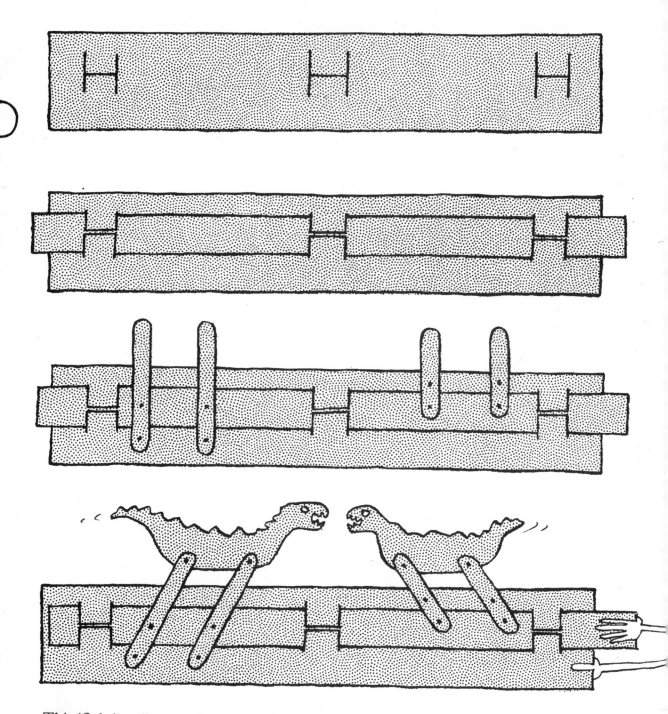

This 'fighting dinosaurs' puppet starts as H-shaped cuts in a strip of card. A thinner strip is then threaded through the 'H's. Join the legs of one of the dinosaurs to the thinner strip and to the card *above* it. Join the legs of the other dinosaur to the thinner strip and to the card *below* it. A single pull on the thinner strip will move the dinosaurs in opposite directions.

TORTOISE TEA COSY

Here's a model which really works for you (if you like your tea hot − or need a present for someone who does). But you may doubt that a tortoise qualifies as a monster? If so, you haven't visited the Galapagos Islands, where tortoises grow to many times the weight of a man. Tortoises can live a long time, longer than anything else with a backbone. They have had a lot of practice. A recognizable tortoise appears in the Fossil Record as long as two hundred and twenty-five million years ago. The tea cosy is a more recently evolved species, but has assumed a very similar shape (this is called 'convergent evolution').

You will need:
Enough cloth to cover the large shape 'A' *four* times
Enough cloth of a different colour or pattern to cover this page
Foam lining *at least* ½ inch (12 mm) thick, enough to cover *both* these pages *twice*
Two beads or buttons
A needle and thread (or a sewing machine)
Scissors

1) Divide the page-sized piece of cloth vertically down the middle *once*, and *five* times horizontally to make *ten* small rectangles.

2) Cut the large shape 'A' *four* times from the larger piece of cloth; *twice* from the foam.

3) Cut the shape of the small cloth rectangle *five* times from the remaining foam.

4) Lay two rectangles of cloth together, right side inside. (If the pattern is clearer or the colour brighter on one side of the cloth − that's the right side).

5) Lay one of the foam rectangles on top.

6) Sew round *three* sides.

These are the legs and head.

(A)

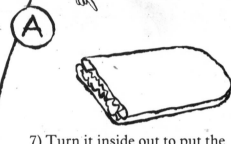

7) Turn it inside out to put the foam inside. Make four more the same way.

8) Stitch toes through one end of *four* rectangles.

9) Stitch a curve for a mouth and sew two bead eyes on the fifth.

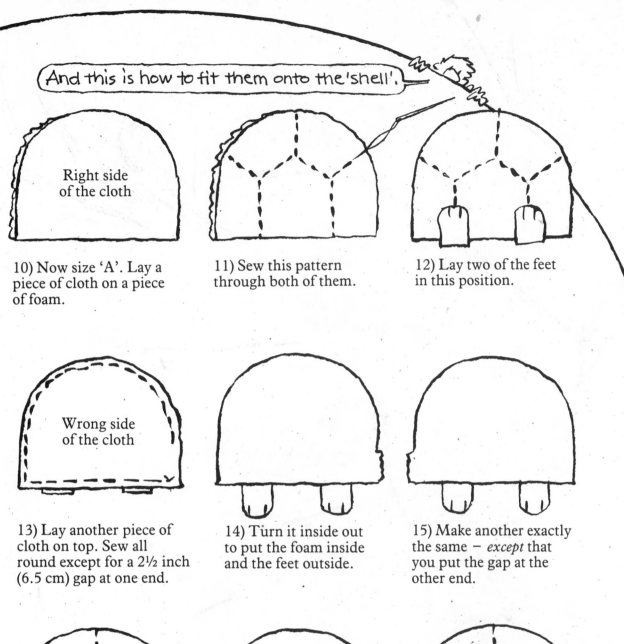

And this is how to fit them onto the 'shell'.

10) Now size 'A'. Lay a piece of cloth on a piece of foam.

11) Sew this pattern through both of them.

12) Lay two of the feet in this position.

13) Lay another piece of cloth on top. Sew all round except for a 2½ inch (6.5 cm) gap at one end.

14) Turn it inside out to put the foam inside and the feet outside.

15) Make another exactly the same – *except* that you put the gap at the other end.

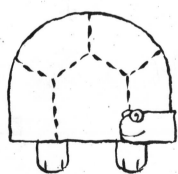

16) Lay one, pattern side up. Lay the head on it in this position.

17) Lay the other one on top, pattern side down, and sew round the curved edge.

18) Turn it inside out and it's finished!

131

You can easily adapt this design to make a stegosaur or a giant armadillo tea cosy. The armadillo needs a tail, which is fixed in the same way as the head. The stegosaur needs not only a tail but also a double row of bony plates along its back. These plates are small foam-filled squares, and are arranged in pairs along the curve between the head and tail. They are attached by the corner at the same time as the head and tail and, like them, should re-appear when the tea cosy is turned right side outside.

Armadillos are mammals and evolved much more recently than stegosaurs. Extinct types of armadillo grew to monstrous sizes. Stegosaurs are *all* extinct, but they evolved more recently than tortoises, which aren't.

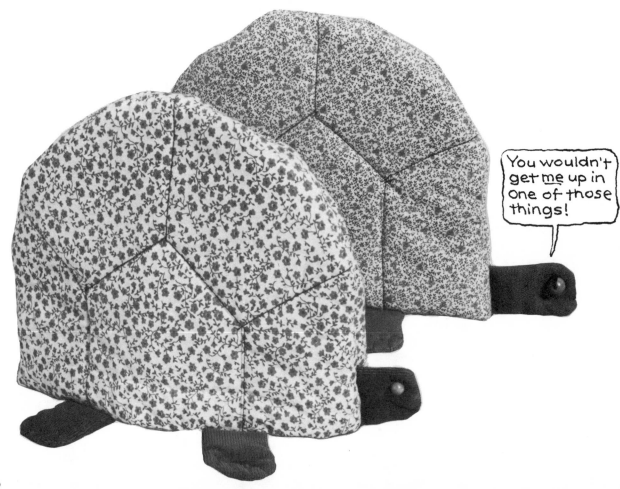

FLYING RHAMPHORHYNCHUS

These flying reptiles had wings each measuring more than the length of a man's arm.
They had sharp teeth and a long tail ending in a diamond-shaped 'tail-plane'.
Make this kite − and make rhamphorhynchus fly again. (It's easier to fly it than say it!)

You will need:
Thin strips of bamboo or split cane (from a gardening centre)
Clear plastic sheet (open up a large clear plastic bag)
Clear sticky tape
Thin black paper (tissue paper is fine)
Masking tape
Light nylon fishing line
A small curtain ring *or* a metal washer
A piece of corrugated cardboard
Two empty plastic detergent bottles *or* lengths of cardboard tube.
A length of ½ inch (12 mm) dowel (at least 2 feet (61 cm) long)
Scissors
A saw

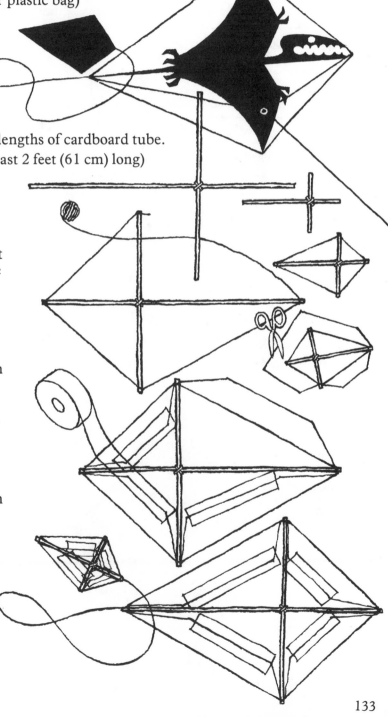

1) Tape or tie a large and a small cross
of cane or bamboo. Make one arm about
a third longer then the others. Make the
small cross at *most* one fifth the size
of the large cross.

2) Link the points of the crosses with
line to make diamond shapes. Bind the
knots with masking tape to hold them in
place on the cane.

3) Lay each cross on plastic sheet. Trim
the plastic to the kite shape, plus a
margin. Snip off the corners so that the
points of the crosses just extend.

4) Fold over and tape the margins. Turn
the kite over.

5) Cut off about 6 feet (2 m) of line. Tie
one end in a non-slip knot at the top of
the kite. Pull the line over the other
end of the kite, draw it back about a
hand's length and tie it on.

6) Tie the end of the line to the top of
the smaller 'tail-plane' kite.

133

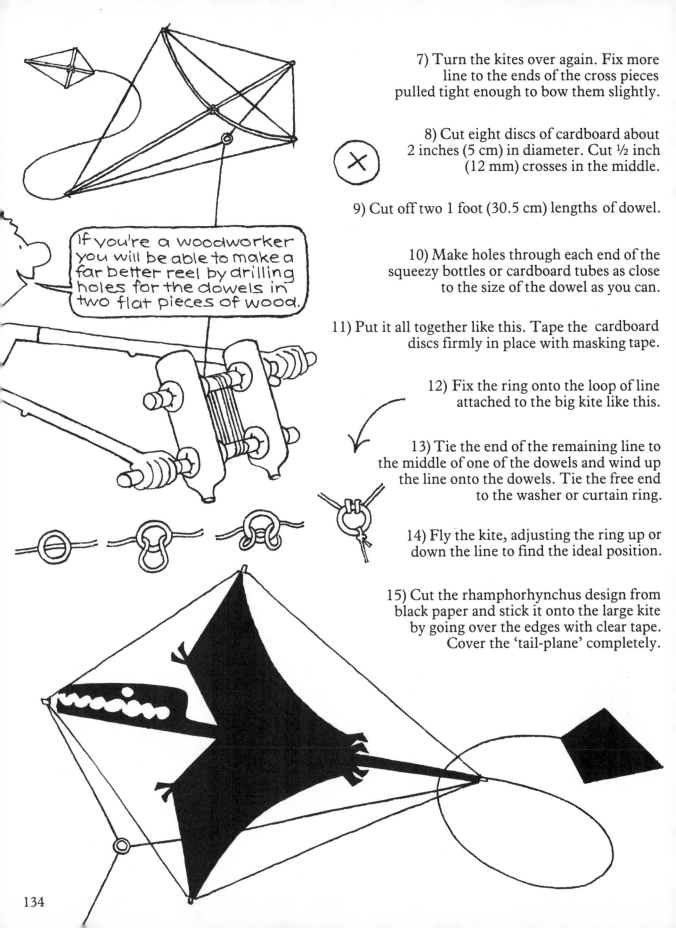

7) Turn the kites over again. Fix more line to the ends of the cross pieces pulled tight enough to bow them slightly.

8) Cut eight discs of cardboard about 2 inches (5 cm) in diameter. Cut ½ inch (12 mm) crosses in the middle.

9) Cut off two 1 foot (30.5 cm) lengths of dowel.

10) Make holes through each end of the squeezy bottles or cardboard tubes as close to the size of the dowel as you can.

11) Put it all together like this. Tape the cardboard discs firmly in place with masking tape.

12) Fix the ring onto the loop of line attached to the big kite like this.

13) Tie the end of the remaining line to the middle of one of the dowels and wind up the line onto the dowels. Tie the free end to the washer or curtain ring.

14) Fly the kite, adjusting the ring up or down the line to find the ideal position.

15) Cut the rhamphorhynchus design from black paper and stick it onto the large kite by going over the edges with clear tape. Cover the 'tail-plane' completely.

If you're a woodworker you will be able to make a far better reel by drilling holes for the dowels in two flat pieces of wood.

You can model a monster in the way a mannequin models clothes. Blue is in this year!

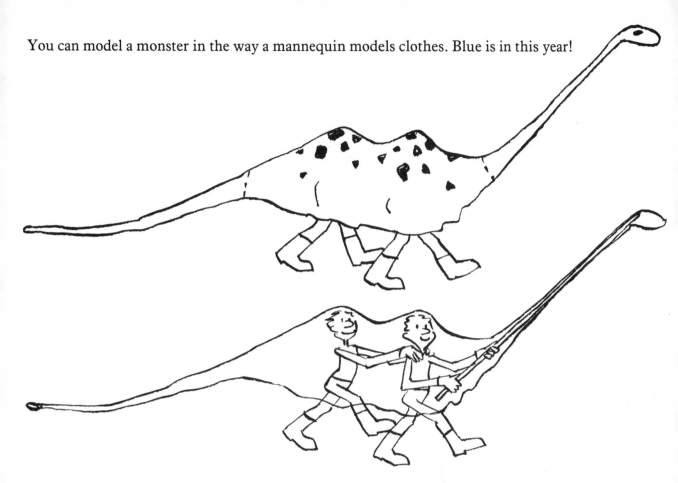

DENIM DIPLODOCUS

You will need:

A broomstick *or* bamboo of a similar length
3 yards (or metres) of blue denim
A needle and thread *or* a sewing machine
Black paint
A small stone (about the size of a golf ball)

It used to be thought that some dinosaurs were so huge that they needed a second brain in the rear end. We now know this isn't true – but this *model* dinosaur does!

Cut the denim into three equal lengths. Lay two together. Sew across one side in the shape of two humps like a camel's back. Leave a gap for the neck and tail and sew up both ends, but *not* the bottom. Trim off waste material about an inch (2.5 cm) from the stitching. Turn it inside out to put the seam inside. Cut two eye-holes in the front of each hump.

Lay the stick on the remaining bit of cloth, about a hand's width from the edge. Fold the cloth over it. Sew a golf-club shape enclosing the stick, leaving the end open. Don't sew too close to the stick. Cut along the line of the folded over cloth. *Don't* trim off the excess cloth this time. Remove the stick. Use it to turn the tube of cloth inside out.

Fold over one edge of the remaining cloth to make a long thin triangle. Sew the long edge. Turn it inside out to make the tail. Drop a small stone in the end to make it drag right.

Stitch the tail into the body. Poke the head and neck (stiffened with the broomstick) through the hole in the front and stitch that in too. Enough of the stick should extend inside to hold. Paint a black spot each side of the head, and a few more of different sizes on the humps to disguise the eye-holes.

Wear this costume with blue jeans and wellies. The person behind walks with both hands on the shoulders of the person in front. Try to walk in step!

TYRANNOSAURUS

It is easier to dress up as a dinosaur than you might think. After all, about half of them stood on their hind legs like you, including tyrannosaurus rex.

You will need:

A cardboard box which fits over your head with a bit of room to spare in front

A bigger cardboard box

Two paper cups *or* the cardboard cores from a couple of loo rolls

Furniture webbing *or* strong tape *or* ribbon

Sticky tape

One of your Dad's baggy old sweaters he has finished with (make sure it's not still his favourite!)

Scissors

Newspaper

P.V.A. (white) glue

A football

A small stone or marble

Squirt glue onto some of the newspaper. Crumple it into the bottom of the smaller box. Push the football into one end, slightly twisting it to make a concave shape. Wash the football and your hands!

While you are waiting for the glue to set, cut down each corner of the larger box in turn, overlap the corners to round them off and tape them in position. Cut off the bottom where it sticks out. Cut a hole in the middle of the bottom large enough to step through. Step through it. Make shoulder straps to hold it at a height at which, if you were wearing nothing else, you would still be decent. Tape them on. Take it off.

Take the sleeves off the sweater. Stitch up the end of one. Drop the small stone or marble into it. Sew it to the bottom of the sweater at the back to make a tail.

Cut some teeth and two nostrils in the end of the 'head' box at the opposite end to the concave hole made with the football. (You will have to look through these, so make them big enough.) Tape the paper cups or loo-roll cores on to make the T.R.'s eyes. (If you want to take the time, you can model a more convincing mask with papier-mâché over a wire frame. Be *very* careful to twist the wire ends away from the inside *and* wind tape round them.)

Wrap the remaining sleeve round your head to make the box more comfortable to wear. Wear the costume with the sweater taped up under the body box.

DIATRYMA

(Birds *also* walk on two legs!)

You will need:
Dad's next oldest sweater
Plenty of old cloth or rags
Corrugated cardboard
A needle and thread
An egg box
P.V.A. (white) glue
String
Yellow tights (optional)
A broomstick

The head shape

Put the broomstick halfway through the neck of the sweater and bind it there with string. Cut the head shape from cardboard and glue it tightly round the free end of the broomstick. Cut up the egg box and add 'eyes' to each side of the head. Tear the cloth into strips and stitch or tie them all over the sweater and broomstick for feathers. Paint the beak yellow and the eyes red with black pupils. Wear yellow tights with this costume (optional).

The age of the killer chicken

You may find it difficult to think of a hen as being very frightening. But a worm has a very different perspective. Imagine a hen towering over you to more than twice the height of a fully grown man. From this worm's-eye view the chicken would look a little like diatryma. Diatryma was an early bird which got the *horse*! Or rather the early ancestor of the horse, and no doubt any other unlucky mammal which got in its way, including *our* ancestors. Diatryma didn't fly. It didn't have to. For some time it looked like becoming permanent Top Predator.

Monster menus

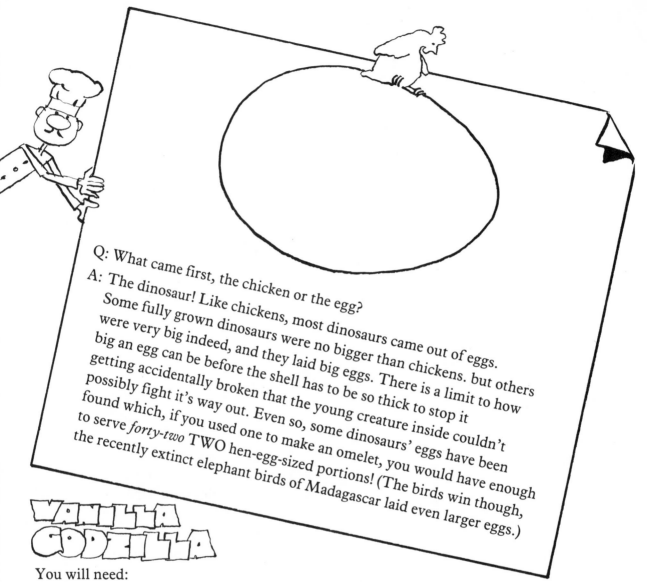

Q: What came first, the chicken or the egg?

A: The dinosaur! Like chickens, most dinosaurs came out of eggs. Some fully grown dinosaurs were no bigger than chickens, but others were very big indeed, and they laid big eggs. There is a limit to how big an egg can be before the shell has to be so thick to stop it getting accidentally broken that the young creature inside couldn't possibly fight it's way out. Even so, some dinosaurs' eggs have been found which, if you used one to make an omelet, you would have enough to serve *forty-two* TWO hen-egg-sized portions! (The birds win though, the recently extinct elephant birds of Madagascar laid even larger eggs.)

VANILLA GODZILLA

You will need:

A large block of vanilla ice-cream

Some ice-cream of a different colour

Split almonds

Raisins

A kitchen knife

A spoon

A fish slice

Two large plates (cool them in the freezer first, this gives you a little more time to work before the ice-cream melts − even so you will have to work fast)

A saucer

A freezer

1) Put about twelve split almonds and a couple of raisins ready on the saucer.

2) Decant the vanilla ice-cream onto one plate. Cut off a large lump and shape it into an oval for the body (use the spoon and knife, don't touch it with your fingers). Lift it onto the other plate with the fish slice.

3) Shape a smaller lump for the head. Put it onto the other plate at the end of the body. Smooth them together with the back of the spoon.

4) Make four short legs and a stumpy tail and join them in the same way. Press the fork into the feet to make toes.

5) Stick the almonds in a row from head to tail, largest in the middle.

6) Stick in the raisins to make eyes and put it back in the freezer to stiffen up. (Pop it in sooner if it is melting too quickly.)

7) Wash and dry the first plate you used and spread a layer of differently coloured ice-cream over it.

8) If the monster is quite firm, slide the fish slice under it and lift it onto the layer of ice-cream on the other plate.

9) Put it back in the freezer until ready to serve.

STRAWBERRY STEGOSAUR

You will *also* need:
Strawberry ice-cream

Make the body, head and legs from the strawberry ice-cream in the same way as the Godzilla version, but this time raise the middle of the back into a taller mound. Put a *double* row of almonds along the back (or you could use dried fruit or chocolate buttons).

DIMETRODON DESSERT

You will *also* need:
Wafers

Make the body, head and legs in the same way as before. Break or cut one of the wafers into about five equal parts. Spread them like a hand of cards. Push the narrower end of the fan into the middle of the dimetrodon's back. (If you make a *big* one, use whole wafers.)

> Putting the plates to cool in the freezer first also ensures that they will fit in after you've made the monster — when it's a bit late to discover that they won't fit!

MERINGUE MONSTERS

You will need:
Icing sugar
An egg
A lemon
2 cups
A tea-strainer
A teaspoon
A tablespoon
A bowl
A fork or a whisk
A knife

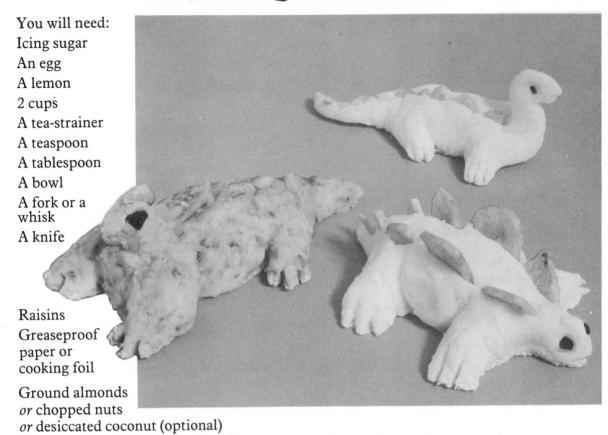

Raisins
Greaseproof paper or cooking foil

Ground almonds *or* chopped nuts *or* desiccated coconut (optional)

1) Break the egg carefully into a cup. Use a clean tea-strainer to lift out the yolk very gently *without* breaking it. Put the yolk into the other cup and put the cup into the fridge to keep the yolk for future use. (It could go into a sponge cake for example.) There must be NO yolk left in the white.

2) Beat the egg white into a stiff foam with the fork or the whisk.

3) Mix the ingredients thoroughly in the bowl in these proportions; one tablespoon of icing sugar to one teaspoon of beaten egg white to about six drops of lemon juice. (Or *four* tablespoons to *four* teaspoons to about *twenty-four* drops, and so on.) If the mixture seems too thin to model with, beat in a little more sugar.

4) Mix in your choice of nuts to taste (optional).

5) Sprinkle a little icing sugar onto the foil or greaseproof paper, tip the mixture out onto it and model some into a simple monster shape. Add bits of nuts or raisins for eyes, spines etc. Make as many monsters as you need for your party.

6) Leave the models to dry overnight. Carefully slide the knife blade under each one to transfer it onto a plate.

(If you are a cook, or can get someone who *is* a cook to help, 2-3 hours in a very cool oven will make these monsters even tastier.)

ALMOND ANKYLOSAUR

Ankylosaurs had to contend with predators like tyrannosaurus. Some ankylosaurs grew as
large as an Indian elephant. They were very formidable indeed with an armoured body
as big as a tank and a powerful tail as long again, ending in sharp spikes or a bony
ball like the thing used to knock buildings down. They could lash this tail round about
knee height to any predator rash enough to get close. There must have been the odd
tyrannosaurus rex who only needed a parrot to give a convincing impersonation of
Long John Silver. Ankylosaurs certainly weren't easy meat − but an almond ankylosaur
can be a tasty snack for a Monster Party!

You will need:
Very clean hands
A packet of marzipan
A packet of split almonds
A pot of apricot jam
Icing sugar
A knife
Two plates

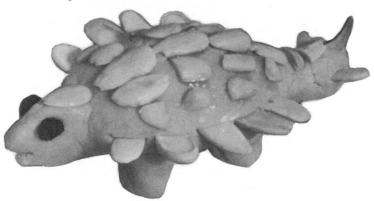

1) Unwrap the marzipan and put it on a plate.

2) Cut off seven small bits of marzipan, leaving one large bit.

3) Mould the large bit into a flattened oval shape and the other bits into four stumpy
legs, a round head and (combining the last two) a tail with a ball on the end.

4) Stick the bits together and finish modelling the shape with your fingers and a knife.

5) Sprinkle the other plate with a little icing sugar and transfer the model to it.

6) Let it harden for a few minutes if necessary, and stick split almonds flat in rows
over the back with the jam. Add a row end on down each side.

SPONGE-CAKE STEGOSAUR

If you can cook an eatable sponge cake you won't need me to tell you how to do it.
If you *can't* − here is what you need: someone to cook you one *or* a shop to buy one in.
The sponge should be round in shape, with or without a layer of jam.

You will also need:
Unsalted butter (or a mixture of five parts butter with four parts white vegetable fat)
Icing sugar (sifted to remove any lumps)

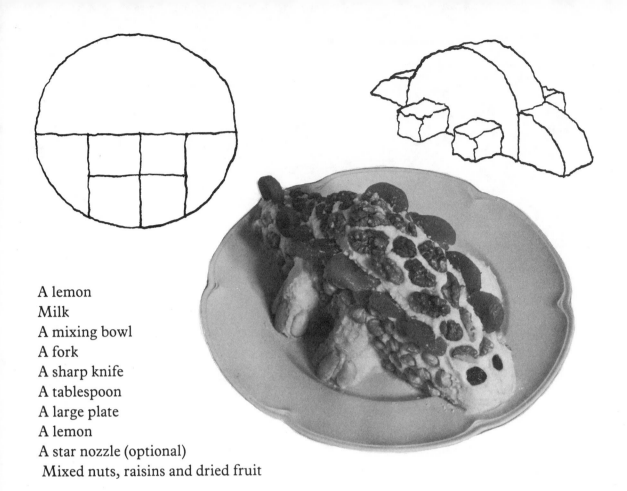

A lemon
Milk
A mixing bowl
A fork
A sharp knife
A tablespoon
A large plate
A lemon
A star nozzle (optional)
 Mixed nuts, raisins and dried fruit

1) By weight, mix one part butter to two parts sugar. Start by gradually mixing *half* the sugar into the butter. Beat a couple of spoonsful of milk into the mixture, then the rest of the sugar. Finally squeeze out the juice of half the lemon and mix that in, drop by drop, stopping before the mixture becomes too sloppy.

2) Cut the sponge across the middle (to make two half disc shapes) and stand one half on the plate on its cut edge. Cut the other half to make four squares and two slightly larger triangles.

3) Add the triangles at each end of the first half on the plate to make a head and tail. Glue them on with some of the butter icing. Glue on two squares at each side for legs.

4) Taper off the tail to a point and round off the head and feet with the knife.

5) Spread a layer of icing over the whole surface. Smooth it to the shape with the convex side of the spoon if necessary. *Or* cover the whole surface with rosettes from the star nozzle, then go over it again filling the spaces in between to give your stegosaur a warty hide.

6) Stick a double row of dried fruit slices into the icing along the back. Add nuts in between if you like (split almonds make lovely toes too) and add raisins for eyes.

Draw a dinosaur
LIFE SIZE!

You will need:

1) This book

2) A very large sheet of paper (brown wrapping paper is O.K.) at least 39 by 16 inches (98 by 152 cm)

3) A roll of sticky tape (if you have to stick paper together to make it big enough)

4) Scissors (if you need to trim it to size)

5) A pencil

6) A large felt-tip pen or paint and a brush

7) Lots of chalk

8) A paved playground

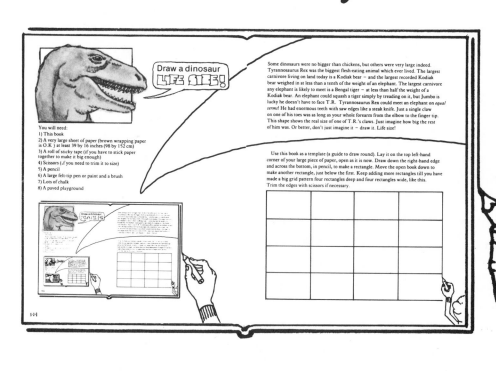

Some dinosaurs were no bigger than chickens, but others were very large indeed. Tyrannosaurus rex was the biggest flesh-eating animal which ever lived. The largest carnivore living on land today is a Kodiak bear – and the largest recorded Kodiak bear weighed in at less than a tenth of the weight of an elephant. The largest carnivore any elephant is likely to meet is a Bengal tiger – at less than half the weight of a Kodiak bear. An elephant could squash a tiger simply by treading on it, but Jumbo is lucky he doesn't have to face T.R. Tyrannosaurus rex could meet an elephant on *equal terms*! He had enormous teeth with saw edges like a steak knife. Just a single claw on one of his toes was as long as your whole forearm from the elbow to the finger tip. This shape shows the real size of one of T.R.'s claws. Just imagine how big the rest of him was. Or better, don't just imagine it – draw it. Life size!

Use this book as a template (a guide to draw round). Lay it on the top left-hand corner of your large piece of paper, open as it is now. Draw down the right-hand edge and across the bottom, in pencil, to make a rectangle. Move the open book down to make another rectangle, just below the first. Keep adding more rectangles till you have made a big grid pattern four rectangles deep and four rectangles wide, like this. Trim the edges with scissors if necessary.

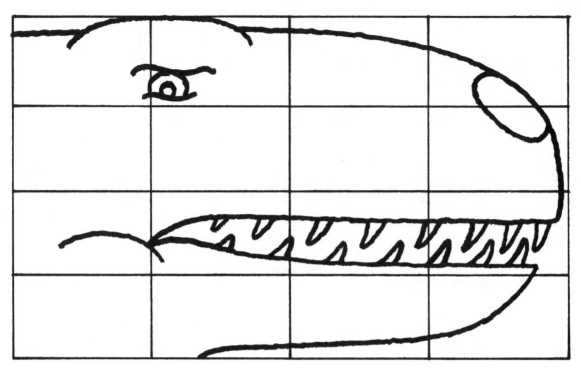

Draw a tyrannosaurus rex's head on your big grid by making the lines of your drawing cross the lines of your grid in the same positions as they do on this smaller version. This is called 'scaling up'. The scaled-up dinosaur head you draw will be life size! Make the drawing in pencil first. When you are sure it is right, go over it in ink or in paint.

Now you can use your life-sized dinosaur head to help you draw the rest of the dinosaur. You can't do *that* at home − unless you happen to live in an aircraft hanger! So lay it out on a very large floor (something like the floor of a gym) or use a school playground.

If you tried to draw it on paper you would need another *fifteen* pieces of paper the same size as the piece you drew the head on. It is easier to use the first piece of paper as a template to chalk a pattern of rectangles like that on the opposite page. Then chalk a dinosaur-sized version of what you see in each rectangle. Why not ask your teacher if you can do it as a school project?

This is a pterodactyl's eye view of a school playground with a life-size dinosaur drawn on it. Even from the height the pterodactyl was flying we had to turn the playground round sideways to get it all in!

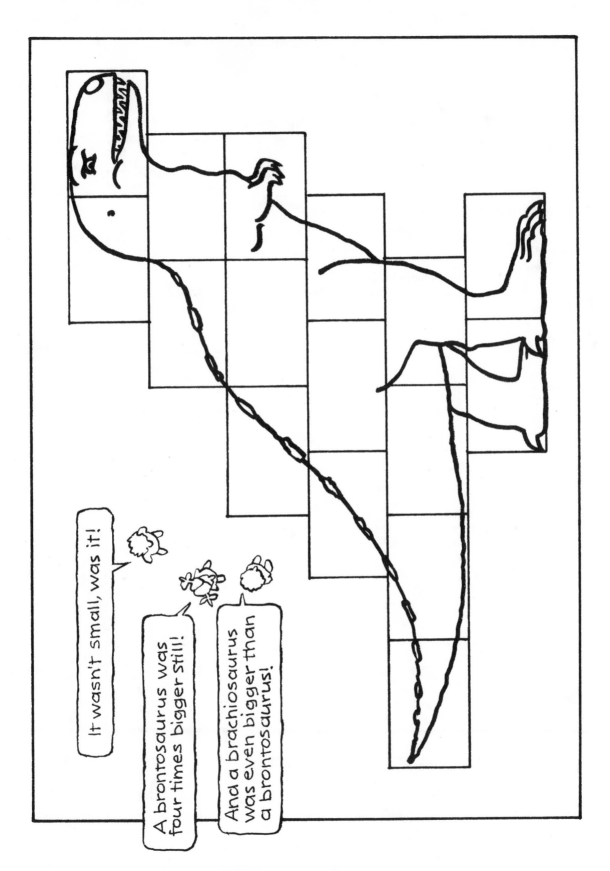

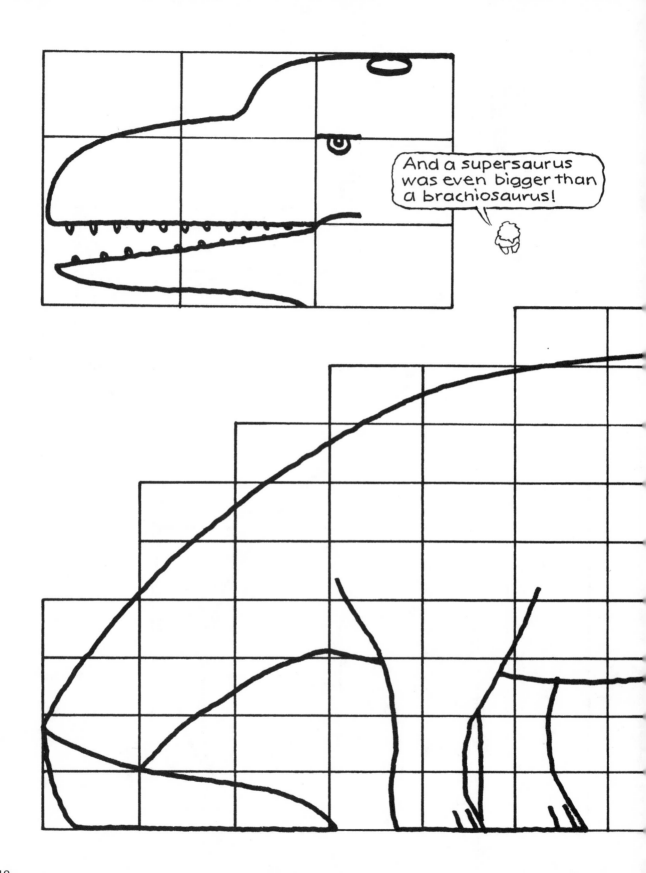

An ultrasaurus, one of the largest dinosaurs yet to be unearthed, had a smaller head but a much larger body even than tyrannosaurus rex. If you want to draw an ultrasaurus life size you need only nine rectangles the size of this open book to do the head — but you need no less than ninety rectangles the size of the head to cover the body!

Like other dinosaurs of this shape, ultrasaurus seems to have been a harmless vegetarian. Harmless, that is, unless it happened to tread on you. When fully grown, its sheer size must have been its most effective defence, like an elephant today. But even more so. A single vertebra from its back would stand almost as tall as a fully grown man!

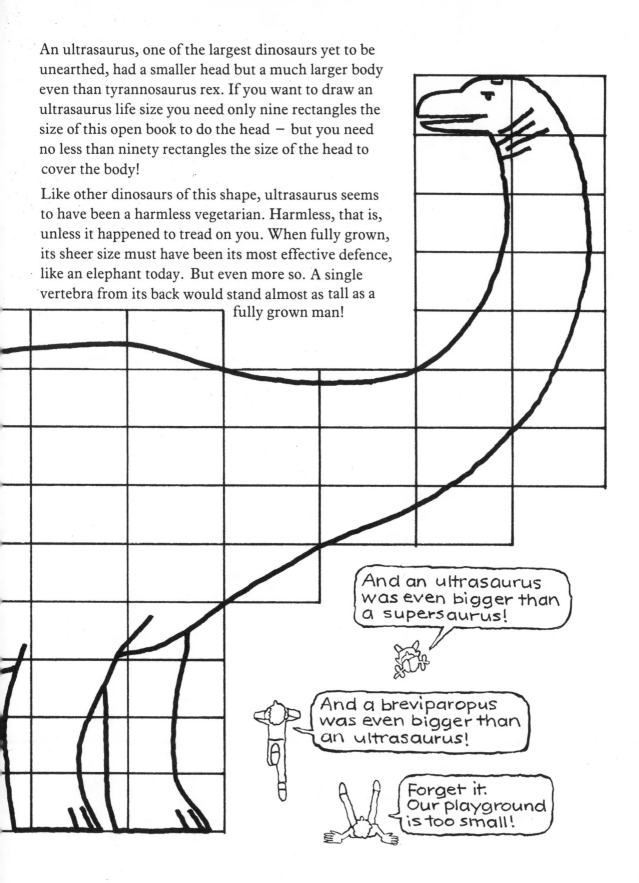

And an ultrasaurus was even bigger than a supersaurus!

And a breviparopus was even bigger than an ultrasaurus!

Forget it. Our playground is too small!

Make a monster diary

You will need:

An ordinary diary (the larger the better, if possible with a whole page for each day)

A pen or pencil

A teacher or librarian (to answer questions or help you find books which will provide the answers)

A library and/or natural history museum (to look for information in)

An ordinary diary records the events of a single year. Make your *monster* diary record the whole long history of life on this planet. To do so, each day in the diary has to represent a period of no less than eleven million years. Here are some important dates to get you started.

Jan 1st

On the page for the first day of January write in the momentous news that living things have appeared (though the Earth is already about five hundred million years old). In the warm, chemical soup of the first shallow oceans now swim microscopic single-celled organisms. Some of these organisms slowly create an oxygen-rich atmosphere. Many are poisoned, others learn to breathe the stuff. All that takes about three thousand million years — which brings us up to October!

October 1st

Now write in the news that some of these single-celled creatures, instead of dividing and drifting apart, have learned to group themselves together into colonies of specialised cells, becoming the first *multi*-celled organisms. You and I are multi-celled creatures — but we aren't due on the scene quite yet. The first multi-celled organisms, in fact, were plants. Animals followed about a hundred million years later (nine days on, in the diary) in the form of soft-bodied creatures, like worms and jellyfish. Some later evolved shells, like clams and crabs. Sexual reproduction, in which two individuals produce a third not exactly like either, allowed evolution to speed up — resulting in a vast variety of plant and animal species.

Nov 17th

The earliest vertebrates (animals with backbones) were fishes, and they appeared five hundred and sixty million years ago — not until the seventeenth day of November in the year of life on Earth.

Nov 29th

The first vertebrates to emerge onto the land (following the plants and insects out of the oceans) were amphibians. They couldn't wander far from the water where, like modern frogs and toads, they had to lay their eggs. Unlike frogs and toads, some of them were giants, who squelched about the steaming swamps we know as the Coal Swamp Forests. The trees in these forests were huge tree ferns, and dragonflies with a wingspan measuring more than the length of a man's arm clattered about amongst them. In your diary, the amphibians crawled out onto the primaeval mud on the twenty-ninth day of November.

These amphibians were the ancestors of the mammals (including us, but we still aren't due to appear for a while) and of the reptiles. Both mammals and reptiles can reproduce away from water. Mammal-like creatures evolved and were very successful until a breed of super-reptiles showed up. They were the first dinosaurs.

Dec 14th

The dinosaurs first appeared about two hundred million years ago. In your diary of life on Earth, this is already the fourteenth day of December. They ruled for the next one hundred and forty million years. During this period, flowering plants first evolved and the insects did so well that soon there were more species of insect than any other animal, which is still the case. A few of the mammal-like creatures managed to hang on in the shade of the dinosaurs, pathetic little insect-eaters too small to make a worthwhile meal perhaps, or maybe scuttling out only under cover of darkness.

Dec 26th

Suddenly, sixty-five million years ago (on the twenty-sixth day of December in your diary) all the many species of dinosaur disappeared from the face of the Earth. And not just the dinosaurs, but many of the plant and other animal species of that time, from the ammonites and giant reptiles of the oceans to the pterodactyls in the air − all vanished in the great catastrophe which is one of the world's unsolved mysteries. It might have happened overnight, or it might have taken thousands of years − a thousand years is only eight seconds in your monster diary.

The mammal-like creatures survived this catastrophe, or enough of them survived to breed a new generation and start to repopulate the devastated planet. (It only takes two individuals after all, if one is of each sex and they manage to meet.) So did a close relative of the dinosaurs. One of the smaller dinosaurs, in fact, which had grown feathers and learned to fly − in other words had become a bird.

It wasn't the smaller birds of the air though who competed with the mammals for the space vacated by the dinosaurs. It was giant, flightless birds much larger and more powerful than a modern ostrich, some with massive heads and beaks. These early birds didn't have to be content with worms − they could run down and kill most mammals which had evolved by that time. There were huge rhinoceros-like things around, but certainly no predator which could pose any threat to these nightmare birds. How did the mammals fight back? Perhaps by attacking the huge birds at the only time they were vulnerable, while they were still in the egg or newly hatched. Perhaps better-equipped mammals were able to evolve in some 'bird-free zone'. Something, at any rate, tipped the balance and the mammals took over the land, diversifying into a great variety of different forms adapted for different ways of life.

Some even challenged the birds in their own element, the air, by becoming bats. Others returned to the oceans, and some of *them* became the largest animals which ever lived, the blue whales, which are bigger than the biggest dinosaur yet discovered. They are still alive today (but for how long?).

Only the most primitive of the primitive pouched mammals, which survive chiefly in isolated Australia, lay eggs. *All* mammals produce milk to feed their young. As a result the young stay with their parents until they are weaned, and so absorb knowledge as well as milk. They imitate their parents, and in some species the parents have learned to teach them. The ability of one generation to learn from another led, when human beings appeared on the scene (yes, we finally arrived!), to language, the steady accumulation of knowledge and what we call 'culture'.

Dec 31st 6.15 p.m. – New Year

Someone more or less recognisable as a human being first appears in the fossil record about two and a half million years ago. This is fifteen minutes after six p.m. on the last day of the year in your monster diary. Human culture eventually led to writing, and writing to written history. Written history has been going on for about five thousand years now. How long is that in your diary of life on Earth? The Mesopotamians and the people we call 'Ancient' Egyptians first started to record history just eighty seconds short of New Year. Christ was born (do you know how many years ago Christ was born?) with only a little more than fifteen seconds of our 'year' of life on Earth still to run. On this scale, the Second World War came to an end only a third of a second ago.

So what is a prehistoric animal?

You can see from all this that to call any animal 'prehistoric' doesn't really mean very much. When people talk about 'prehistoric monsters' they usually mean dinosaurs but, for millions of years before history came to be written, we would recognize more or less familiar deer, antelope, elephants, cats, kangaroos etc. Long after the dinosaurs became extinct, strange mammals which we *wouldn't* recognize appeared and evolved into more familiar forms, or became extinct in their turn. Some of them rivalled the larger dinosaurs in size, and were as fearsomely armed. You wouldn't want to meet a mammoth or a sabre-toothed cat down a dark alley! There have been beavers bigger than pigs, pigs as big as rhinoceroses and rhinos larger than elephants – as well as elephants which, fully grown, wouldn't come up to your waist and hippos standing no higher than your knee. All of which lived far too late to meet a dinosaur. The dinosaurs were very dramatic and varied and stayed on top more than three times as long as the mammals have yet managed, but they were only one chapter in the long story told by fossil remains.

Filling in the gaps in your diary

See if you can find out which day the plants first emerged from the sea onto the land (don't forget that each 'day' in your diary is eleven million years). See if you can find out which day the insects emerged, and when they learned to fly. See if you can discover when Pangaea, the super-continent, broke up, and what the effect was of part of it drifting over the South Pole, and of the isolation of Australia, and of South and North America becoming linked. Find out when the flowering plants first appeared, and where to put the Ice Ages in your diary, and how many Ice Ages there have been. The first Ice Age occurred about two hundred and fifty million years ago, and there have been no less than nine in the last million years alone!

On the scale of your diary you will find it hard to squeeze in all the Ice Ages, let alone many of the events of human history. But if you can find out when they lived you can fill the pages with drawings of the different species of animals, and set them in the many landscapes that appear and vanish in the record of the rocks long before history came to be written.

Make a monster scale

You will need:
Chalk and a paved playground
This book

Make a monster time-scale in the form of a continuous strip so that you can see everything in perspective. Mark the events of evolution on it in their appropriate positions. Use these two pages as the end of the time-scale, stretching back from the present day for the past five million years. To lengthen the time-scale, just keep tracing round the book, open as it is now, and moving it on to make a line of rectangles, each representing another five million years.

If you want to go back all the way to the very beginning of life on this planet, four thousand million years ago, you will have to chalk a strip of no less than seven hundred and ninety-nine rectangles − then add this book to the end.

If you would like to start your scale with the appearance of multi-celled life forms, one hundred and ninety-nine rectangles plus this book will be enough. If you would prefer to begin with the first amphibians you still need to draw ninety-nine rectangles. But perhaps the best place to start would be with the appearance of the dinosaurs, which took place about two hundred million years ago.

In that case your will have to draw the outline of this open book only thirty-nine times (which, with these two pages at the end, will still make a line 50 feet or nearly 15.5 m long − your playground might not be big enough even for that!).

Nearly all the animals which appear in this book in the form of models lived within this period and can be placed on the scale. Apart from the model fossil trilobite and ammonite only three date from an earlier period. Can you guess which three? One is the sail-backed dimetrodon, the other two might surprise you. They are the familiar crocodile and the tortoise, both still with us. Another dates from much more recently − the mammoth undoubtedly met our ancestors, and was probably exterminated by them.

Why not start by drawing up a table like this? Then you can work out the proper order.

	Where found	How old	Life style	Size
Dimetrodon	N. America	250 million years	Land carnivore	39 feet (12 m) long
Stegosaur	N. America	135 million years	Land herbivore	22½ feet (7 m) long
Tyrannosaur	N. America/Asia	97 million years	Land carnivore	19½ feet (6 m) tall
Brachio				
Tricera				
Trilobi				
Ankylos				
Mamm				

Dimetrodon (notes)
Sail-back pelycosaur from the Lower Permian. There was also an herbivorous version, edaphasaurus, which could have been the first land-dwelling herbivore. It was once thought that their huge 'sail' helped them navigate the swamps and lagoons they lived in. Now it seems more likely that it was a quick-start mechanism, the sail being full of small veins so that, if the creature stood sideways to the sun in the morning, its blood would warm quickly, giving it the jump on its unfortunate prey. The plant-eating version, presumably, was better able to escape predation. Clever, but not clever enough to compete with the dinosaurs when they came along. Its descendants survived only as small, obscure insect-eaters. But these insect-eaters survived the dinosaurs, to evolve into elephants, and bears, and you.

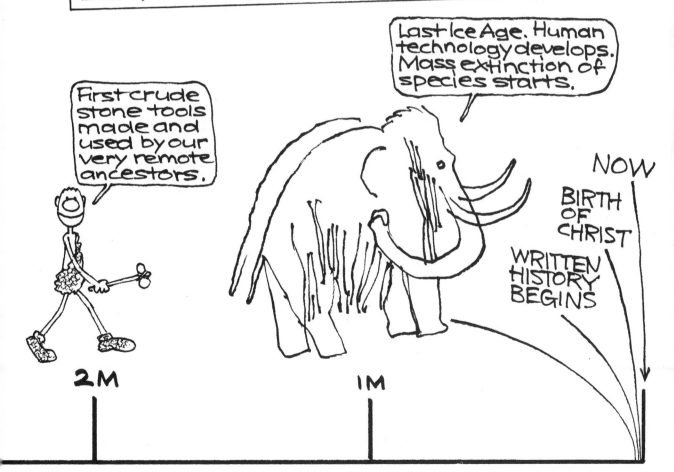

The extinction game

Try to find the answers to these questions. You might solve the world's greatest mystery!

You will need:

A sheet of paper

A pencil or pen

These might help to find some of the answers:

A teacher, a librarian, a natural history museum

(If you have borrowed *this* book from a library, please put your answers on the sheet of paper, not the book!)

Here are some of the ideas people have come up with already to try to explain the disappearance of the dinosaurs:

They just wore out: Wearing out is out. Worms and fish and frogs are still with us and they evolved long before the dinosaurs. In fact all species are related and none is older than another because life isn't constantly re-created. We all date back to the same primaeval slime.

Disease: Disease is unlikely to have accounted for *every* species of dinosaur. *Plus* all the other species which went at the same time. Including the pterodactyls, the great sea lizard and the ammonites.

Plants evolved poisons in self defence: The same goes for poisons as for disease.

Climatic change: There is no geological evidence of global deserts or global Ice Ages. Temperature actually determines the sex of some living reptiles, and a change of temperature might produce all males or all females! But what about the ammonites? When land covered the South Pole because of Continental Drift, seasons probably became more extreme. Trees started to drop their leaves in winter, which would be tough on leaf-eaters. But this never happened in the Tropics and − what happened to the ammonites?

Mammals ate all the dinosaurs' eggs: If the eggs were such easy prey surely the dinosaurs would never have lasted more than a hundred million years. Anyway, what happened to the ammonites?

Meteor strike or nearby super-nova: Very difficult to prove or disprove. Certainly either could be sufficiently catastrophic. A large meteor or a comet smashing into the earth, for example, might throw vast quantities of dust into the atmosphere. The following few weeks or months of continual darkness and cold would have made life difficult on land and in the sea. Even clobbering the ammonites! Though seeds, and insect eggs, and fish already frozen in ice, and trees which had lost their leaves in winter, and hairy little mammals huddled hibernating in holes might survive. It's a good theory − but it's not the only possible way to explain these effects. . . .

Q Does evolution usually work as (A) a steady, slow progress or (B) a series of dramatic spurts in response to sudden changes in the environment? Tick the appropriate box.

☐ (A) ☐ (B)

Q Did mankind's comparatively large brain (A) develop slowly and steadily over millions of years or (B) appear quite suddenly on the evolutionary scene?

☐ (A) ☐ (B)

Q If tools were used *before* flint axes and arrow heads, what material would most probably have been used by a creature which was in the habit of pulling on branches to reach fruit and nuts and sometimes found the branches coming away in his hands? What would happen to this material that wouldn't happen to stone?

☐ Sand
☐ Wood
☐ Metal
☐ Plastic

Q Would this material have been better or worse than stone for making each of these items? (Why is there not an age named after it, as there is after the stone tools our ancestors made?)

☐ Fires
☐ Spears
☐ Boats
☐ Bows and arrows

☐ Sledges
☐ Wheels
☐ Ladders
☐ Roofs

Q How long is it since the first Stone Age?
How long is it since the extinction of the dinosaurs?

Stone Age.......................
Dinosaurs ....

Q Would you expect more, or less, evidence to survive from the forgotten Wood Age (whoops, sorry!) than from the last days of the dinosaurs?

☐ More ☐ Less

Q Most fossils are discovered when they weather out of rocks. If *not* discovered they soon erode away themselves. At any one time most fossils have either worn away or are still deeply buried. What are our chances of finding even those individuals which *do* get fossilized?

☐ Good ☐ Poor

Q How many individuals manage to get fossilized? (A) One from each generation of each species? (B) One from each species? (C) Not even one from each species?

☐ (A) ☐ (B) ☐ (C)

Q Which is more likely to get fossilized? (A) A species living in water or swamps. (B) A species inhabiting higher, drier ground?

☐ (A) ☐ (B)

Q Would a species developing technology be more likely to be found in (A) swamps or (B) higher, drier areas?

☐ (A) ☐ (B)

Q Would some scientists of the remote future, finding fossils of modern frogs and crocodiles, imagine our technological civilization?

☐ Yes ☐ No

Q Were the dinosaurs all (A) lumbering, cold-blooded reptiles which laid eggs and took no further interest in their young or (B) active, possibly warm-blooded creatures which cared for their young and, in some cases, might have borne them alive?

☐ (A) ☐ (B)

Q Human hands were free to learn to use tools because people began to walk upright. Can you think of another type of animal which habitually walked erect? ....

Q Is pressure to evolve co-operative behaviour and intelligence greater upon (A) big, powerful, well-armed species or (B) smaller, more vulnerable species?

☐ (A) ☐ (B)

Q Might some smaller species of dinosaur have scampered nimbly about in trees, evolving grasping hands and binocular vision – just as our ancestors did millions of years later?

☐ Yes ☐ No

Q (A) Did the comparatively big human brain evolve before our grasping hands and binocular vision or (B) did our hands and forward-looking eyes, by allowing us to manipulate objects, encourage our brains to develop?

☐ (A) ☐ (B)

Q Soot deposits have recently been discovered associated with the end of the dinosaurs, suggesting vast fires 'many times the effect of a nuclear bomb'. Some scientists see this as supporting the meteor-impact theory. Which do you think would be the most likely to cause the damage of many nuclear bombs?

☐ Meteor impact
☐ Atomic war

Q If some such disaster wiped us out today, which do you think would be likely to survive into the future (A) fossils already deeply buried, (B) anything on the surface now or (C) fossils of anything evolving afterwards?

☐ (A) ☐ (B) ☐ (C)

Q If a nuclear war happened to break out between Gondwanaland and Laurasia, how many years would be likely to pass before another nuclear war became possible? (If you don't already know, find out what happened to Laurasia and Gondwanaland.)

.... years

Q At what other period in the history of the world have so many plant and animal species become extinct as at the time the dinosaurs disappeared? ....

Q If the answer is the present day — why is it happening today? Is it (A) direct persecution by people, (B) loss of environment due to human population pressure, (C) pollution due to human technology or (D) all three?

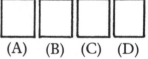

(A) (B) (C) (D)

Q Are the different species surviving today now going the same way as the dinosaurs?

No Perhaps Yes

Q Who are the monsters now? ....

This is only a theory to add to all the others, what some people call a 'model'. Making models is how we try to understand things better. The trouble usually begins when people start to believe that their particular model is reality.

What might the physical attributes of an intelligent dinosaur have been — if one ever existed? Why not make it a project to draw up a specification and model one? Ask your teacher.

It is obvious to anyone who ever opened an atlas that South America once broke off from Africa — but even after someone thought up the Continental Drift theory it was years before the 'experts' accepted it.

When a creature evolves which is capable of changing its environment instead of being changed by it, when medical science allows fit and unfit alike to survive and breed, then there is no *mechanism* for further evolution. What do you suppose can happen then?

The Children of Earth (A model of future evolution)

'We have explored the empty galaxies', said the traveller, 'the billions of burned out worlds − only to discover this grim law. Intelligence is the biological equivalent of Going Nova. Living forms, wherever they appear, always evolve towards a superior intelligence. It has great survival value, at first, but it is a time bomb, ticking away down the ages. When culture and artefacts appear, on an evolutionary scale it is an end, not a beginning. Time has run out. Less intelligence is needed to destroy a world than to preserve it. The lesser degree of intelligence necessarily evolves first, so intelligent life forms are doomed to extinction at their own hands. Our computers tell us that we alone escaped this natural law not by one chance in a billion, but by one chance in infinity. Yet you, the Children of Earth, have also survived your childhood home to populate the habitable worlds of your galaxy!'

'We too are the creatures of evolution', replied the representative of those living on the planet. 'Twice Earth was brought to disaster, and has been for many aeons now a dead, radio-active hulk. Life evolved there, as elsewhere, crawled on its ancient sea floors, swam in its waters, crawled out onto the land, swam freely again, buoyed up by the insubstantial air. At the time of the second destruction, a bird, which men called a swift, could fly for three full Earth years, feeding and sleeping on the wing, before in its maturity it returned to the surface to nest and lay its eggs, bound to the land as amphibians are bound to the water. But another creature, which men called a bat, bore its young alive. These, clinging to their mother's fur and drawing life from her until mature enough to fly themselves, eventually gained complete freedom from Earth's surface. Naked wings with no covering of feathers became increasingly able to absorb energy directly from sunlight, and bats became independent of the failing supply of insect food. Flying ever higher above the destruction unleashed by men, they grew at last free of even the thin upper air, free to fly on the solar winds.'

'And you are descended from these bats?'

'The bats, if they exist, are gone forever into the darkness beyond the galaxies. But at first, long, long ago, they visited planets circling alien suns . . . and the bats had lice.' The representative worked leathery mouthparts long starved of blood.

160